"I tempted all His servitors, but to find
My own betrayal in their constancy
In faith to Him their fickleness to me
Their traitorous trueness and their loyal deceit"

Francis Thompson

Anthony Brady - 2016

Anthony Brady

Nothing Matches
But It's Home

Book 4 of the series
"Scenes From An Examined Life"

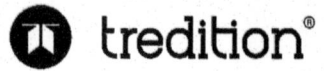

© 2017 Anthony Brady
Cover: Petra Schubert
Editing: Petra Schubert

Publisher: tredition, Hamburg, Germany

ISBN
978-3-7323-9803-4 (Paperback)
978-3-7323-9804-1 (Hardcover)
978-3-7323-9805-8 (eBook)

Table of contents

About the Author

Anthony J. M. Brady was born in 1940 in London. He retired in 1994, having completed a career in local government as a Principal Officer Team Leader with the London Borough of Camden, from whose Chief Executive's Department he had been seconded to the Department of Health & Social Security (Resettlement Centres) for 15 years. In 1997, he moved to Northern Ireland and lives in Brockagh, Tempo, Co. Fermanagh.

A Communitarian, he participates in part-time voluntary work involving social reconstruction, advocacy, renewal and reconciliation. His first writing in print was an essay in the London Chest Hospital Staff Magazine: Shakespeare and Medicine (1964). His first letter to a newspaper appeared in the Catholic Herald and this led to a series of polemical exchanges in its letter's page about the American/Vietnam War with the writer John Braine (1969/70). His first writing fee was for a book review: Caring on Skid Row by Anton Wallich-Clifford – the founder of The Simon Community, commissioned by The Catholic Herald (1974).

Subsequently, (1981-1986) he had letters published in The Catholic Universe, Hackney Gazette, The Guardian, The East Ender, The East London Mercury and The Greenwich Mercury on topics such as Apartheid; Drug Addiction; Homelessness and social justice issues. Many of his letters on topical issues have appeared in The Fermanagh Herald and The Impartial Reporter.

The Guardian printed four of his letters (1987-1990). One highlighted the threatened closure of a service for adolescent mentally ill people at The Maudsley Hospital; another two were arguments against reduction of hospital provision in London and the fourth objected to the euthanizing of the first person in England to have feeding methods legally withdrawn to assist his death.

A Paper, entitled helping the Resettled Person with a Relapsing Drinking Problem, was published by the Charity, Good Practices in Mental Health. ISBN 0 948445297

Tony began to send out creative work for the first time in 2003. A short story: 'Sister of Mercy' was published by the weekly magazine "Ireland's Own" and in 2004 an historical profile about Angela Burdett-Coutts: Queen of the Poor, was published by the bi-monthly magazine "Ireland's Eye". Both publications are popular in Ireland and the United States. Since 2003, he has had published (in anthology) numerous poems in various publications under the aegis of Forward Press: Anchor Books, Triumph House and New Poetry.

Dogma Publications have also published his poetry in anthology. Other works comprise "Castle Coole - Millennium Evocations - A house tour in verse", "Thank You! Miss Hutchinson - Collected poems", "Cast Out Remorse!" - Short Stories, Essays and Commentaries.

Acknowledgements

While writing this book, I received great encouragement from former inmates of *Saint Joseph's Home, Enfield*. They have read drafts of my work and made comments in an Epilogue, serving to validate through their own experience, these recollections that recall my years 1945-1952.

Though dealing less with personalities than I, the late *Norman Taylor* has described faithfully and accurately the prevailing social conditions revealed in historical data through his researches in the archives held by The Crusade of Rescue's successor organization, The Catholic Children's Society. Norman has also revealed much concerning the scarcely documented life of girls in other Homes who were the separated siblings of boys at St. Joseph's.

Peter Landsborough compiled the St. Joseph's Home, Enfield, **Glossary of Slang**. It contains over a hundred expressions: he began this during the 1960's using his abilities for writing and flair for correspondence with former Enfield boys scattered around the world; he has also met many former Enfield boys through his yearly attendance at the Salesian Old Boy's Association Re-Unions at Blaisdon.

Mike O'Brien RIP 2017 - a published poet – has written numerous letters to me recalling his Enfield experiences and commented on my own. A series of searing published poems – Intimations - illuminate his early life in St. Joseph's Home and his transition to a Gloucestershire farming experience. In keeping with his contemporaries and later generations of boys – who share an unbreakable line of friendship developed over half a century – Mike has described in a poem this bond as inspired by *"The long years of harshness, the sudden change from grief gave common cause that bound us with as strength beyond belief"* **(The Brotherhood)**.

Michael McKenna has been encouragement itself. His letters, comments and opinions on drafts I have sent him, have been enormously moving.

Norman, Peter, Mike and Michael, these my memories are the sum of your parts. In the words of the Blaisdon School song: *"Rivet fast the friendships made in youth at boyhood's home..."*

I thank particularly *Sammy Hayes* who was an Enfield and Blaisdon contemporary. I am indebted to *Carol Roper* of The Catholic Children's Society, who inherited the records of The Crusade of Rescue, for her assistance and acquainting me with other source material to aid my researches. *Sister Joan* – Archivist – The Daughters of Charity, Mill Hill, London, graciously provided the St. Joseph's Home and associated photographs.

The regular contact with *Fr. Sean Murray SDB, Charles Springett and Terry O'Neill* through their work for **The Blaisdon Old Boy's Association** has been inspirational.

For their technical help, I thank the staff of the public libraries in counties Fermanagh and Tyrone: *Mairead McKenna, Amanda Hamilton, Doreen Dunwoody, Fivemiletown, Gerry McKenna, Lisnaskea and Ken Newman, Mobile Library Services.* A special Thank You to *John Cloughley*.

Finally, none of the books in this series would have been produced without the dedication of *Petra Schubert* as my editor.

Synopsis

The "*Scenes from an Examined Life.*" is an autobiographical series. In 1939, a child is conceived out of wedlock in Northern Ireland. The protestant father is married with 10 children. To avoid scandal the catholic woman moves to London. She is forced to abandon her six-month-old child in a London Cathedral. The Crusade of Rescue, a Catholic benevolent society, arranges fostering and in the years 1945-1952, the child is cared for in St. Vincent's Home, Feltham and St. Joseph's Home, Enfield, Middlesex, run by the Daughters of Charity of St. Vincent de Paul.

The mother was disfigured by fire in a childhood accident. The Orphanage Sisters discourage mother and child contact saying she frightens him. He is told that his mother has died in an air raid and his father in the war. He is led to believe that his mother's accident was a penance and that when he is older he will be disciplined by men in expiation for her sin. The boy exists in an often harsh, confusing and unforgiving environment, subjected to many humiliating examinations of personal effects and frequent "examinations of conscience". He experiences various forms of abuse, is bullied and often lives in fear. Even so, he makes fun of things with his companions and makes lifetime friends.

Though the mother cannot see her child, she lives in the house of a Jewish couple as a nanny until their 3 children grow up: two become doctors and the third a pharmacist. She stays on with the couple until they retire. Meanwhile, the child is moved when 12 years old (1952) to a residential vocational training school in Blaisdon, Gloucestershire, which is run by men: The Salesian Fathers of Don Bosco.

The boy is treated kindly by the priests and lay brothers, and his progress in school leads the Rector to propose moving him to one of the Salesian colleges. He opts to leave when 15 and is given a job on the school farm as a stockman. The farm manager, Fr. Dan Lucey becomes a surrogate father to him: when 17, he learns of his origins and experiences a spiritual crisis. Fr. Dan encourages him to visit Lourdes "to take his mind off himself". The experience there and subsequent four pilgrimages motivate the young man to resolve to dedicate his life to others.

On the last one, he works with a Belgian Jesuit Père Raoul Lievens, who becomes a spiritual mentor. Against the advice of Fr. Dan, he leaves the farm where he has worked from 1955-1961 and goes to live in Belgium. From working in a TB sanatorium at Mont-sur-Meuse, Ardennes, he is accepted as a student in The Institute of Tropical Medicine, Antwerp and qualifies to work in the former Belgian Congo.

Books of the series "Scenes From An Examined Life":

Book 1 *"Of What is Past"*

Book 2 *"Blaisdon Made Me"*

Book 3 *"Near And Dear To Someone"*

Book 4 *"Nothing Matches - But It's Home"*

Chapter 1 – Two Gentlemen Of Stepney

There were two clubs on the north side of Victoria Park Square in the 1960s: *The Assumption & The Repton*. On Tuesday nights, I helped out in the former, which provided a variety of activities to teenage boys and girls. The latter club - boys only - specialised in providing boxing activities for adolescents and young men. In the Assumption you could always recognise the girlfriends of the boxers: they hardly participated and kept to themselves, while waiting to be joined by their boyfriends when training finished at *The Repton*. I was supposed to be a bouncer if necessary, but rarely, if ever, exercised that authority, as both clubs closed about the same time at 10.pm usually noisily but peacefully.

Once a year, *The Repton* staged a Gala boxing evening where it show-pieced its established and rising stars. The East End society *en toute* patronised this event. A regular attender at Assumption and a nephew of the Repton's Warden invited me to be his guest and the following week - although not at all keen on boxing - I went along. It was a fine Autumn evening as I closed up the club and stepped out of the *Augustinian Priory* where *The Assumption Youth Club* was situated. The lights from the rear of *The Museum of Childhood* glowed through a fine evening mist and glinted on the metal gates of the closed green space that was bounded by Paradise Row, Bethnal Green Tube Station and the Church of St. John on Bethnal Green.

Inside the Repton, I was soon spotted by the Warden, *George Layton*, and he formally introduced me to the members of the Committee seated at his corner table: "Tony, I would like you to meet the Chairman. May I have the pleasure of introducing the Club Secretary; can I acquaint you with our Head Trainer?" and so on. Through the tobacco and cigar smoke, I could barely see the other guests indicated in the official programme: principal cup and purse sponsors seated at the other raised corner tables who, with the packed standing room only crowd, watched the ring. It being the Interval, the youngest trained boxers - slim white vested, baggy shorted - and none-contenders on the gala bill - entertained the crowd with sparring feints and punching their weight into the padded fists of their trainers.

Presently, George, signalling to a short, heavily built man nearby, said I should meet two ex-members who were present. He exchanged a few words with the man whose face I could see showed much evidence of boxing experience. Whenever I see the character Odd-Job in the James Bond film *Goldfinger,* I am reminded of him: squat build, bow-tied, oriental in appearance, mainly because of the punches to the eyes he had taken at boxing to the highest level. These would have been in regular York Hall appearances: a nearby venue where the East End boxing professionals contended. "Odd-Job" silently indicated that I follow him. He made no effort to negotiate his way to a corner table; the crowd seemed to part instantly at his presence until he was approached by another bow-tied and similarly obvious pugilist. They exchanged words, which in the general hubbub, I heard as "catholic club", "geezer", "no trouble," "Yeah! Right!"

With one escort now before me and another at my elbow, I soon arrived at a table at which six men were sitting. The nearest was watching the young boys in the ring and seemed to be moving his body in unison with their movements. We waited as he would not be distracted. Then the leading escort leaned over and said: "Ronnie, Reggie, this is Tony. Ee's aw'right!" A voice at my elbow, Odd-Job's, emphasized: "Yer, geneleman!" I shook hands with Ronnie who stared past me immediately towards the ring. Next, I shook Reggie's outstretched hand. "George" he said indicating a man wearing a fedora hat who proffered his hand which I shook. Then a voice boomed "Boothby" as greeting, and we shook hands. At this point, a bell sounded the end of the Interval and a fanfare announced the next bout on the bill. There being no spare space at the table "Odd-Job" efficiently led me back to my original place.

As the evening progressed, my table set filled me in on the characters I had been introduced to. My escorts were indeed professional boxers having come through the Repton stable. *Ronald* and *Reginald Kray* were also ex-Repton members of the club, having learned boxing there as boys and in their teens. Later, they were to be infamous as the gangster *Kray Twins*. At that time they loved gangster movies. "George" was *George Raft* - a famous Hollywood actor who played gangster roles. In contrast to the likes of *James Cagney* and *Edward G. Robinson,* actors in the same genre, Raft never knocked women about and acted the part of a gentleman killer. As the announcer intoned "My Lord, Ladies and Gentleman!" few present guessed it was *Lord Boothby* sitting with the Krays.

All of these personalities presented prizes as the bouts were fought through the different weights. The "purse" was largely raised by paying members of the public and added to by the distinguished guests. All monies raised went to paying the running expenses of the Repton which, in its day, was the premier boy's boxing club in London's East End. The Club was founded in-the 19th Century and promoted by Repton Public School in Northamptonshire. During the long summer breaks boys and masters lived in the impoverished East End. Working as social missionaries they fostered what was to be called "muscular Christianity" through clean living, godliness and teaching the noble art of boxing.

Various Public Schools also set up Missions in The East End. On the bill that Gala Night were bouts between members of Boy's Clubs such as Eton Manor Hackney, Hailybury Stepney, Oxford and Cambridge House were other University Settlements in the area. Young, rough, tough and uncouth boys and young men became gentlemen and fought within the Marquis of Queensbury Rules.

Many years have passed since that evening encounter with *The Kray Twins*. They have become a distinct part of London's East End criminal folk-lore. I have heard that comparisons and contrasts are made between The Krays and today's villains in which the Twins are cast in favourable terms. That they loved their mother and were kind to old ladies are sentiments expressed in the common currency of clichés. As by chance, I happened to be presented to them, I am particularly intrigued by resonances in the observation: *"The Krays! Real Gentlemen! They never killed anyone without being introduced to them first!"*

Chapter 2 – Dear Sir - Things Are Getting Rougher

D ue to "welfare" training (1966/68) as door attendant at *The Priory* in *Victoria Park Square, Bethnal Green* I had built up an informed knowledge of the movements of homeless people, and memorized the wide geographic range of the previous addresses they gave, when I had to note them in the Caller's Book. Whenever someone said "NFA", I would press them as they were drinking the tea and eating the sandwich that I had prepared and invariable the name of a hostel would come up. I circled these places in my A-Z of London under a heading called *Emergency Accommodation*.

On those many occasions, when a homeless person was desperate on a winter's day to have accommodation for the coming night, I was able to issue one of Father Hilary's pre-signed notes to a night shelter or other temporary accommodation. This promised payment for the first night. In those days, it was possible for a homeless person to book in for one night at a *Salvation Army Hostel*, then take the booking receipt on the following day to the designated (for people without a settled way of life) *National Assistance Board Office* at Scarborough Street, near Aldgate East, and have the stay extended by voucher. In this way, they obtained a foot-hold which could lead to a casual job, money and some stability.

At the local *London Supplementary Benefit Claims Offices*, which replaced the NAB, a single homeless person was given short shrift due to the very rigid rule that every claimant had to have an identifiable address to satisfy consideration for entitlement to benefit. For example a rent book, utility bill, or post office book would need to be produced to confirm a local living connection. If any of these appeared to be bogus, the claimant was asked to wait while a member of staff walked or drove round to the claimed address and checked its veracity. When the claim proved to be false, the police were called and an arrest made.

Though never equipped with these requirements, the homeless single person was supposed to, according to the rules in the manual known as the A Code - the social security officer's bible - be seen officially, a statement of need taken and then a small cash sum awarded to get them to the Scarborough Street Office or the nearest Reception Centre. The local Office I worked in (1970/74) was situated in Hackney, Lower Clapton. Aldgate was three miles distant while the Reception Centre, situated in Peckham, was over six miles. The reality of this specified treatment was the homeless person kept waiting in reception all day and at 3.30 pm closure time sent on their way without assistance.

One morning, before going on my house visiting round, the office Manager *Mr. Norman* delegated the post opening duty to me. This was a very strict procedure. The postman was met and any signatures required were recorded and the post was laid out on a large table. Then, the office post box was unlocked and its contents included for opening. A clerical officer CO stood by, observing these initial procedures, then watched while an executive officer EO opened each envelope or package as the Manager looked on. A letter knife opened each corner: the envelope or container was spread out flat by the CO; payment order books and the sometimes cash and cheques removed and logged and all correspondence set aside and laid in a pile.

Then, the EO date stamped every piece, read every letter and flagged all official ones for referral to the various sections of the office: payments, pensions, sickness, unemployment, liable relative, fraud. These were then passed over to the clerical officers known as searchers, who carried them away for manual linking around the office. Finally, the Manager and EO studied the letters written by members of the public and those which were sent in anonymously. It was decided by the Manager what action should be taken. Those that were signed and addressed were put up for an urgent visit.

This particular morning, a Monday, I had completed the procedure and all that remained was two unsigned handwritten letters and a scrap of paper, which had been retrieved from the office letter box: one detailed a grievance that a neighbour (name supplied) was "living off the social" and working and "something should be done about it!"; a second described how a working man was living with a woman (named) who was "drawing" on the grounds that her husband had left her; on the scrap of paper were scrawled the words: *"Dear sir things are getting rougher."* There was no address, nor name.

Mr. Norman said *"Make an early morning un-notified visit tomorrow to the claimants named in the two missives and as for the scrap paper note, put it in confidential waste!"* That kind of completion was supposed to be done and witnessed in writing by us both but he was suddenly called away, so I said I would log it with my signature and one of the searchers when they returned. He went off saying he would anyway check and verify the post-log next morning. I studied the words and sensed somehow that they were a cry for help. Presently, *Grace Giveaway*, the principal searcher came by. I told her I was concerned and would she have a close look at the writing. She recognized it immediately and said *"That's Victoria Adams... Two kids... In care... A complete nutter... In and out of The Homerton*, probably in there now. I'll get you the case-paper!"

The following morning, I made my two early visits and called by at the block of council flats where Victoria Adams lived. There was no reply. A resident a few doors down on the same landing saw me and said that that the person I was calling on had gone out at about nine o'clock. I continued on my rounds to complete twelve notified visits and returned to the office at about two o'clock. The first person I met was Grace: *"Norman's sent out a taxi looking for you! The police and social services have been down. Adams is dead. She's been found on the railway at Hackney Down. All they want is the case-paper."*

A month later, I had an appraisal review with *Mr. Norman*. Before going up to his office, Grace mentioned that a letter had come in about me and she had read it before Mr. Norman had took it with him. The appraisal went well apart from a grumble from my Visiting Section Head that I was too generous with giving emergency and extra needs grants. Then I was asked if I wished to raise any matter? I mentioned that we did not deal properly with homeless callers and I referred to the relevant sections about how they should be treated. Mr. Norman stared at me then said *"You have to learn Brady that we here are not social workers! Our job is to make payments swiftly and fairly in response to local needs. What I will do though is put you in charge of dealing with these people. But as you are one of our best visiting officers you will have to combine this area with your present responsibilities. That's all - apart from this"*. He picked up a paper from his spotless blotter. He perused it and laughed.

"This is one for the Regional Staff Magazine! It's from a Miss. Eager, E5, whom you recently visited. Your visit was obviously welcome as she writes here in this letter addressed to me." 'Dear Sir, the visiting officer who came to see me was very nice and gave me very good treatment. He tested the bed and sent me a grant for a new one. I am very grateful to be now expecting a baby. Can I please have the same visiting officer next time? Thank you.'

From then on, I was to deal regularly with different homeless callers and Mr. Norman was pleased that they never returned. This was because I had the A Code means at my disposal and was able to use the accommodation information supplied to me by the homeless themselves. The reason they never returned was that when I telephoned a particular hostel and reserved them a bed, I told them that I would later check that they turned up and note our records accordingly.

One of my most valuable aids was the BF2. This was a system that nationally circulated descriptions together with aliases of claimants whose identities had proved to be false; vulnerable people, listed as missing on police files; dangerous people who had assaulted staff and those with warrants out for their immediate arrest for obtaining benefits by false claims. The code for each Office where claims had been made and the date of the most recent claim was marked and indicated where the case-paper could be obtained. These were entered on a pink BF2 card and placed in the hundreds of filing trays secured in steel lockable cabinets. No new claim was ever set up until a cross check was made to see if a BF2 was in the filing system. Every day, BF2 data arrived for entry and filing by the searchers.

With this system, all that was required was a telephone call using a code number to actually access the case-paper information and command its transfer for arrival in 24hrs. Every three months, the whole filing system was "weeded" and every case-paper without a fresh claim in the past two years or was no longer "live" was destroyed. The BF2s remained *in situ*. Every homeless person I dealt with was screened against the BF2 system. The only ones that ever checked positive were mentally ill and sometimes under section, having detached themselves from hospital care. At such times, the hospital was contacted and the social services notified.

This regular involvement and activity relating to homeless people brought me into contact with all the London Social Security Offices, The Reception Centres and the two seven days a week emergency offices in central London and Glasgow. I also had a whole range of dealings with various forms of accommodation facilities and services run by Charities for homeless people. One caught my attention when it advertised in *The Catholic Herald* for an experienced welfare Administrator: a particular requirement was practical knowledge of *obtaining social security benefits for the homeless*. I applied.

Chapter 3 – Tasks Unfinished – Dreams Denied

I began work in *Providence (Row) Night Refuge*, 50 Crispin Street, Spitalfields, Stepney, E1., in June 1974. My appointment as Administrator was wide ranging. The purpose built Refuge was opened in 1868 by a none sectarian Charity founded ten years earlier by a *Monsignor Gilbert* (1827-1895) who was the *Vicar-General of the Arch-Diocese of Westminster* and *Administrator of Westminster Cathedral*. It provided free shelter for hundreds of men and women who slept rough in the area at that time. The original management committee members had invited a group of Wexford based Sisters of Mercy to assist them and the working association proved continuous. User numbers had reduced but the original Aims survived.

The Night Refuge - a Grade 1 Listed Public Building - was built over an extensive basement area and consisted of two separate entrances into reception areas at ground level which were linked to dormitories on the first floor. The Sister's Convent home was integral to the building together with a primary school, 9 homeless family furnished flats and two residential hostels accommodating 40 "business girls." It occupied in its entirety an island site a stone's throw from *The City of London Corporation* owned *Spitalfields Fruit Market*. "*Petticoat Lane*" was just round the corner and *Brick Lane* a couple of turnings. In sight was *Nicholas Hawksmoor's Trinity Church* where in its Crypt the *Church Army* ran a residential service for *Crude Spirit Drinkers*. The connection with Westminster Cathedral was maintained and the *Cardinal Archbishop* was a supportive benefactor.

Shortly before I arrived, the *Cardinal* had completed an extensive private visit, in which he considered all aspects of the Charity's work. He then called in the Management Committee and expressed a number of serious concerns. He said that it was bordering on scandalous that the Refuge was customarily closed for six months of the year. He told them that representatives of the many church based charities in the area had complained that it was virtually impossible to communicate and co-operate with the Refuge. While praising the thrift of the Members who had made it the richest charity of its kind he implored them to spend money - pointing particularly to the need for housing. The Cardinal said that his contacts with officials of the Supplementary Benefits Commission indicated a willingness to fund the costs of the Night Shelter provision if the practice of allowing only working men in was ended. Finally, the Members were virtually instructed to advertise and recruit a Company Secretary and Welfare Administrator with social security benefits experience.

Cardinal John Heenan visits St. Joseph's Hospice for the Dying – Hackney 1970

The most pressing immediate challenge I faced with *Roger Shelmerdine*, the newly appointed Secretary, was the intention of *The London Fire Department* to imminently issue a Closure Order on the whole complex due to its repeated and frustrated efforts in obtaining satisfactory safety precautions. The Chief Fire Officer noted that on his last inspection, the Convent fire extinguishers were hidden behind fire doors whose closure springs were removed and the Mother Superior had told him that there was no need to be concerned as *"The Refuge and Convent were completely in the protection of The Virgin Mary."* He noted that yet again the roof level escapes which ran from the Refuges to the Sister's accommodation locked and bolted on the convent side. The *Men's Refuge Warden* had informed him that *"the men have to be locked in at night as a precaution against them invading the Convent!"* The comprehensive survey with minimal specified positions for wall fire alarm switches and fire alarm points was set out on a Schedule that failure to comply with would lead to closure and heavy fine.

The urgency of this was resolved by commissioning Chubb Fire & Safety Co., Ltd to install the necessary protection and a benefit for me was the opportunity to acquaint myself fully with the building while the work was being completed by August. The Fire Certificate was issued and I toured the building with *Reverend Mother Mary Fidelis*, who assiduously sprinkled Holy Water on all extinguishers and break glass boxes. Both Rodger and I realised that the building was no longer suitable to purpose, and studied closely the file of "feelers" from City Companies that had expressed an interest in buying the free-hold. Another factor was the aging and declining Community of *The Sisters of Mercy*. An additional concern was that the Order was embarked on a process of renewal and having to decide where to concentrate its apostolate, which embraced work in hospital nursing, education and social work. It was also experiencing losses of its younger Sisters.

The Management Committee met only three times a year and expected an outline brief from me by September as how to proceed while mindful of the Cardinal's concerns. My Plan of Action addressed these directly. The Refuge will be open all year round. An Open Door policy will operate with an earlier opening at 4.30pm instead of 6.30. The Refuge will be used as an address for users to claim National Insurances Benefits. A medium stay form of accommodation would be introduced to the Men's Refuge. Priority of referral to a designated number of Refuge beds would be given to local homelessness charities. The staff will be increased by 100%. The dormitories will be upgraded to cubicle accommodation.

The Consultation Paper produced devastating results. The key staff resigned and *Mother Fidelis* indicated that there was no support for it in the religious community. It was then that I learned that neither she nor they had been party to the earlier discussions with the

MC and his *Eminence*. I sent my Plan to the Chairman and was summoned to his office.

Gerard White told me he worked in "futures" as an expert in investments and held a top position with a premier finance company in the City. He masterminded the growth of Providence Row's investment portfolio and over 20 years and had made it the wealthiest and foremost of the registered Charities of its type. He played the Stock Exchange astutely and regularly placed tranches of the Charity's bank interest on the Money Market with brilliant success. A veritable master of the universe of finance, he admitted that he knew nothing about homeless people, much less about how to manage their welfare and care. I sat with him as he faced a line of television screens connected to various parts of the financial empire. Every now and then, he would pick up the receiver of any from an array of telephones and say "Buy" alternating to "Sell" or "Hold". He advised "Do what is necessary but don't alarm the Sisters!" and turned his attention to his all consuming passion. Later that year, I was to meet his wife who told me that her husband had retired some years back then, the following week, he had returned to his old office and rented a corner there so as to continue his money making.

My meeting a couple of days later with the local *Social Security Office Nelson Street Manager, Mr. Alan De Medici* went extremely well. I took my (also departing) personal secretary *Miss. Lawlor** with me and she took Minutes. We agreed that anyone coming to the office with an official letter (drafted and tabled) stating that they were in the Refuge would be sent a pocket money payment plus a voucher for Providence Row to recover the nightly costs of their food and shelter. All claimants other than pensioners would require either a Form B1 from The Labour Exchange or a Medical Certificate.

Soon, I attended a monthly meeting of the combined umbrella body of all the charities in the area known as No Fixed Abode. I told the twelve representatives of organizations such as The Salvation Army, The Church Army, The Methodist Bow, East London & Whitechapel Missions, Spitalfields Crypt, St. Botolph's, Algate, The Simon Community and so on, that Providence Row intended to commit itself in partnership with their work. Mother Fidelis looked forward to welcoming them. Affiliation followed in due course.

During this induction period, I met with *Cardinal Heenan* and over dinner with him and *Monsignor Bartlett* - Cathedral Administrator - and brother of *Anthony*, a Providence Row MC Member, his eminence assured me of his support and told me about his renewed hopes that the Charity was going to play an effective part in the combined church social work in East London. In his post-prandial colloquy, Cardinal Heenan informed me of the growing social justice outlook of relatively new organizations such as The Cyrenians, The Catholic Housing Aid Society, The Simon Community, St. Mungo's, No Fixed Abode and (the mooted) Home Office, Tower Hamlets Council & GLC Spitalfields Renewal Project. He noted how they recruited their key staff through press advertisements and said that this signalled an end to the traditional practice of making appointments to Providence Row by patronage. In that observation, though I was not aware of it then, lay the seeds of my destruction.

At the end of the evening, the *Cardinal* said that he would bless me. I knelt before him and he laid his hands on my head, then raising me to my feet, I bowed and kissed his ring. *"God Bless you! - you, a Crusade of Rescue child have come in your prime to the rescue of our greatest Charity"*.

The next four years were marked by inspiring success and the realisation of all the Charity's plans. *Providence Row* built 12 houses for disadvantaged families, established a long stay and resettlement project for Refuge users, agreed on a housing quota with Tower Hamlets Housing Department. The former primary school was converted into a women's hostel and the foundations laid for a purpose built long stay hostel for women admitted from the Refuge. The Homeless Families Unit was fully refurbished. The Refuges became a hub of co-operation of referral-in and move-on into rehabilitation on a London-wide scale. A doctor provided a surgery for Refuge users. The Nuffield Foundation awarded its largest ever grant to fund a Research study into Homelessness and Schizophrenia. The Charity's Annual Reports and MC 1974/79 Minutes testified the effectiveness of the twin track approach of Secretary and Administrator working together and the combined support of The

Sisters of Charity. The money flowed in. *My life-time career was assured. Then, suddenly it was over.

Roger retired prematurely. His post was passed unadvertised to a friend. The Chairman wrote when I was on holiday, saying that the newcomer would take overall charge of operations. I learned that he had no previous experience in homelessness. I complained to the MC, was ignored and took my complaint to the top. I refused to accept the situation and never returned to my post. My former supporter was dead and so was Mother Fidelis. I was an embarrassment to the new Cardinal. Nevertheless, he advised a legal settlement for "Constructive Dismissal" which I accepted with compensation. The Committee, as individuals, supported my stance but was immovable in backing Gerald.

"I tempted all His servitors, but to find

My own betrayal in their constancy

In faith to Him their fickleness to me

Their traitorous trueness and their loyal deceit"

(From "*The Hound Of Heaven*" by Francis Thompson)

The exception was *Charles Bellord*, the MC's lawyer, whose family had been connected with managing the Charity since its inception. I had reason to consult him when two Irish sisters - not nuns - were arrested for alleged placing of bombs in London. One of their legal representatives had approached Mother Fidelis with a proposal that they be bailed to the Refuge. Seemingly, the principle of *sanctuary* was advocated. The legal opinion from Charles Bellord clarified this as a misapprehension. About the same time, a *Commander Roy Habershom of The Special Branch* telephoned me to warn that the Refuge was under surveillance due to its use by potential IRA bombers. Enquiries had established that most of the kitchens in (the likely to be bomb targets) West End Gentleman's Clubs in Pall Mall and at the Ritz and Savoy Hotels casually employed Irishmen who resorted to hostels on a regular basis.

Although the feared backlash against Irish people during that period never materialized, it was this particular group that suffered due to the inevitably tightened security measures. The special but unofficial Department of Employment Offices in Denmark Street & Mortimer Street, W.I. where from 2.00 am men queued for a metal disc entitling them to be directed to an establishment for a day's work from 5.30 am closed more or less overnight.

Charles Bellord had the good grace to telephone me before the paperwork arrived that I was, in grateful recognition of my services, being awarded a year's salary in advance and that Providence Row would contribute to a pension until I was 65. Not only did I lose my post but my home as well because I lived in the scheme with the eleven disadvantaged families as an unpaid family assistant and adviser. It was an encouraging compliment when many of the denominational charities in the area offered to create a post for me, which on principal I could not accept. Thanks to the *Bow Methodist Mission*, I moved to an empty vicarage in Bow, and aged 40 with a wife and three young children determined to build on the wreckage as I considered the tasks unfinished - the dreams denied.

* Miss. Lawlor long term office assistant was very knowledgeable on the history of Providence Row and told me that the poet Francis Thompson (1859-1907) quoted above, who in 1893 wrote *The Hound Of Heaven,* spent time in the dormitory of the Men's Refuge when he was destitute and addicted to laudanum: a tincture of alcohol and opium. She also told me that it was an historical fact that in 1888 two of Jack-the-Ripper's 5 victims: *Catherine Eddowes* and *Elizabeth Stride* had sheltered in the Women's Refuge in the weeks prior to their deaths. She advised me that, though I had big money plans, never to overlook the small kindnesses of donors and *"Don't forget to be nice to Doctor Morrell!"*

The following September, *"Winny",* who had come as a homeless person from an orphanage to the Women's Refuge fifty years ago and lived in a room above the dormitory, brought me tea and asked if I was *"In or Out"* today? She always sat in a tobacco smoke haze in a tiny reception room by the door to Gun St. where she filtered out speculative callers: *"Ee's not in!"* - *"Ee's out in the van!"* *"Ee's round the Men's entrance at 4.30!"* and so on ...came in to my office and said an elderly gentleman, calling himself a doctor, was waiting to see me.

The doctor gave his name and explained that he is making his annual pilgrimage to Whitechapel where, in the 1940s, he met his wife when he was a medical student and she a nurse at The London Hospital. He had come up to Liverpool Street Station from his home in Sussex with a gift of a jar of his home-made jam for the homeless which he then handed to me. Over a cup of tea *Dr. Morrell* told me that in all the years that he had visited, he had never been inside the Refuges while his wife, now dead, had helped out with serving the Refuge Christmas Day Dinner for hundreds of people years ago. He was truly delighted when I gave him an extended tour of the whole place and escorted him to the convent to meet Mother Fidelis. After chatting with the good doctor, she bade him goodbye and gave him a bottle of malt whiskey. He continued his yearly visits - always with a jar of jam. I made sure to make a fuss of him.

Although I never returned to Providence Row, I heard that another crisis, involving The London Fire Service, was brewing unless a comprehensive upgrade with smoke detector and sprinkler system was installed. It was estimated to cost £60.000. Not long after that on reading the Wills, Legacies and other Bequests column in The Times, I learned that Doctor Morrell had left that amount to Providence Row Night Refuge & Home, Crispin Street, London, E1.

Chapter 4 – Beds

The Providence (Row) Night Refuge (Crispin Street) is a drawing by *Arthur Ellis*, circa 1890s. The homeless women are seen crowding into the light and the warmth. A quantity of straw was strewn at the entrance and in the hallway. Unclear above them and cut deep into the stone is the word WOMEN. The Convent of Mercy at the right end of the building is unlit except for a gas light at its door.

On the left side of the picture, a Hansom cab stands in Raven Row, later Artillery Row which leads through to Middlesex Street - "Petticoat Lane" - and Liverpool Street. A dense queue of homeless men wait to be admitted to the Refuge. Above the entry door also cut in stone is a similar heading MEN. The outer gate - a sliding one - was opened just wide enough to allow admission of one person at a time. When 140 men had entered, the gate was closed and scores of men were turned away to seek shelter and food as best they could.

After saying Grace before Meals at 6.00pm, two Sisters of Mercy attend a night's intake of 42 men in the Men's Refuge basement dining room circa 1976. 12 men had found

work from the Refuge and were in "lying time" i.e. waiting for their first week's wages, which were paid after two week's work. 11 were in various stages of alcohol addiction. 6 were "dry" and moving on to residential recovery projects. Six had been discharged into home-lessness from London prisons that day. Two were "escaped" mental asylum patients, traceable by the hospital pyjamas under their clothes. Three had just arrived in London. Two had wives and six children being put up in the Women's Refuge. The remaining four were "barred" from other hostels.

Not shown is a welcoming open fire, which was always lit before 4.30pm opening time. Earlier, other helping Sisters would have kitted out their guests with fresh clothing and footwear from the store. The Sisters had a calming effect on the men. It seemed to be a special consolation to them to know that in their poverty and distress they still had a woman to wait upon them. There were basic washing and shower facilities in the dormitory. Reading matter and TV were available until 9.00pm. Most of the guests were in bed within an hour of having supper. Once admitted to the Refuge, going out and in was not permitted. A hot breakfast saw them on their way in the morning.

The view of one of the Women's dormitories is towards the convent wall and doors. 102 beds were provided. The women got in from the foot of the wooden bedstead under which their possessions were stored for the night. The mattress was covered with an easily cleaned "American cloth" - a kind of sailcloth. The bedcover,

recommended as the warmest and healthiest by Doctors, consisted of one rug made from four sheepskins sewn together which could also be cleaned read-

ily. The two small windows are set in the walls of the nun's cells where night watch was kept and users could summon help by tapping on the glass.

The Men's Dormitory - *"The Poor Man's Hotel!"* contained 45 beds. The metal partitions were installed in 1976 and hung with fireproofed curtains. Sleepers, who had precious items, laid them under the mattresses and as an extra precaution rested the feet of the head of the bed in their footwear. A staff member slept in an adjoining room and a "trustie" could let users out as early as 5.30 am for casual work in Spitalfields Fruit & Vegetable Market.

The Women's Reception area and Dining Hall decorated for Christmas in the early 1900s. The bowls are quite large. In the early days a controversy about gruel or cocoa being preferred by the guests was resolved when Dr. Gilbert took a show of hands and the decision was in favour of the latter.

It was customary for the *Cardinal Archbishop of Westminster*, to help with the serving of the Christmas Dinner. In their turn, Cardinals Wiseman, Manning, Vaughan, Bourne, Hinsley,

Griffin, Godfrey, Heenan and Basil Hume all helped with slicing the fowl and presented a small gift to the hundreds of homeless diners.

The *12 houses at Aylward Street*, Stepney, E1 have been developed by a newly created Providence (Row) Family Housing Association.* Their building - a mile from Providence (Row) - was prompted by Cardinal Heenan and they were occupied as permanent tenancies by needy East London families. Later, when the children grew bigger the open play area was converted to individual back gardens.

*Ironically, the development was achieved with virtually no cost to the Charity due to the site being donated and government grants available at the time.

Chapter 5 – Following Jack London And George Orwell

My departure from Providence Row opened an opportunity to study, and in 1978 I enrolled at *The Alcohol Studies Centre, Paisley College, Lothian, Scotland*. A one year foundation course, leading to the Diploma in Alcohol Studies, demanded a Dissertation with an original Action Research component. So, with the aid of the Centre's Director Dr. Bill Saunders, we designed a Prevalence of Alcoholism & Alcohol Related Problems Survey, using an alcohol dependence questionnaire, developed by The Maudsley Hospital Institute of Psychiatry. It was down to me to identify the area for the research and arrange access to the survey group, which was to be targeted on men and women living in hostels for the homeless in London's East End.

My objective, I discussed with *Dr. Richard Smith*, the then Administrator of The Bow Methodist Mission, and leading advocate for social and housing justice for homeless people and hostel dwellers. He and co-workers were handicapped for many years by the lack of empirical research based knowledge about the hostel dwellers. Richard, anticipating the uniqueness and originality of this research venture, designed a secondary questionnaire. This would elicit a raft of demographic data to strengthen neighbouring campaigns, aimed at promoting access to local authority housing, which was denied to hostel dwellers.

The character of *Tower Hamlets* (formed by the amalgamation of the Metropolitan London boroughs of Bow, Poplar, Bethnal Green and Stepney) was derived from its position on the banks of the Thames downstream from Tower Bridge, its position close to the City, and its role as an erstwhile major port and manufacturing centre. For historical reasons, it emerged as a predominantly working class area. Development of industry, commerce and housing was rapid throughout Victorian times, and while industry and commerce had experienced major economic fluctuations of expansion and contraction the momentum of growth, change and demand in housing had experienced a continuing and contemporary impetus. In keeping with most inner London boroughs vast areas of slum and tenement accommodation, which were a characteristic of housing in Tower Hamlets, had been displaced by extensive Council low-rise estates and low ground density high-rise units of housing. Such development was a notable characteristic of housing in an area where the bulk of all dwellings were Council owned and where more than half of which was owned by The Greater London Council.

An exception in those changing patterns of housing was the accommodation, traditionally and currently used by the hostel-dweller in the area, in which my survey was to be conducted. Change there had been, but change that bore little or no comparison with those, which characterised the housing of the indigenous population. Indeed, had Jack London and George Orwell - writers who had actually stayed in some of the hostels - when researching material for their respective books The People of the Abyss (1903) and Down and out in Paris and London (1933) revisited them in the 1970/80s they would have found the living conditions they had experienced virtually unchanged. I was to meet most of my respondents in large open dormitories and in the exception (Tower House) interviewed.

By the mid 1970's, the byword on the subject of hostels, indeed an evocative catch-phrase was "Enough is Enough", which reflected an almost unique harmony between prominent members of both the Tower Hamlet's Council and community spokesmen. For the most part, they were at logger-heads over all other social conditions in a locality, which has been described as the most deprived area of London. Some slight indication of the changes in housing, which had affected accommodation for the hostel-dwellers in the area, was the decline of the small lodging-houses, of which there were over 2,512 being visited regularly by the Borough's Medical Officer of Health in the late 1930's. Such establishments lodged numbers of men and women from five to twenty and disappeared in the post-war years. However, the decline in that type of accommodation was not matched by a decline in the number of hostel-dwellers. A census of common-lodging house dwellers in 1939 revealed a gross figure of 1,385 while in 1979 the gross numbers remains virtually static at 1,800.

Although it did not lie within the remit of my survey to specify the historical changes, which made the hostel-dwellers an easily identifiable group within the area, it was useful to acknowledge an important difference between its patterns of movement and that of the indigenous community. It was one of immigration and emigration. In the indigenous population, it has been a characteristic to emigrate to the New Towns with stimulus from the housing authorities. In the hostel-dweller an unchanging characteristic was their inclination to immigrate into the area: the stimulus, being cheap accommodation near to a pool of cheap labour. Another important reason for this immigration into the area, and particularly pertinent to the approach adopted by my survey, was the anonymity that the hostel-dweller's way of life endowed.

Before illustrating in some detail the group of hostel-dwellers, which formed the subject of the survey, it was necessary to identify and place in a particular perspective two other groups: one, central to the hostel group as a whole, and another at its periphery. Within the area of the survey, there existed a number of alcoholic recovery projects, all non-statutory, which provided varying levels of recovery alternatives whose provision extended to a total of 100 beds. Their approximate turnover of clients in any year was 570 people. For the purposes of identifying, the prevalence of alcoholism, a reasonable indication of such prevalence, could be inferred from an aggregate of clients which these agencies served. Such an inference, however, would be disjunctive, for these agencies, while drawing the bulk of their clients from the hostel population in the area, also operated on a metropolitan-wide network of in-referral which extended well beyond the Borough's boundaries.

The second group consisted of - on the most conservative estimates - 150/200 homeless alcoholics who were believed to be sleeping rough at all times of the year, within the area of the survey. The existence of such a group was not peculiar to the London Borough of Tower Hamlets. Analogous groups were easily identifiable within the neighbouring boroughs and at their interfaces. In any considerations of prevalence of alcoholism within the area, it was nonetheless a group of major importance, largely because of the distortions its presence conveyed on impressionistic notions of prevalence. The most references to alcoholism in the community via the local media emanated from observations about their Skid Row phenomenon, so any prevalence of alcoholism, which was identifiable, was reduced to judgements about this stereo-typical group: the homeless alcoholic.

To the public at large, homeless alcoholics were barely discernible. They either merged into the landscape, which they inhabited, or were rapidly removed from it. But to be homeless and an alcoholic was to be endowed with a supreme visibility, particularly in the eyes of the police. They were more likely to be caught when committing an offence or when in possession of illegally obtained goods. Because they were homeless, their drunkenness was public. Because they were drunk, they were most certainly refused a place of lodging. Consequently, they were most susceptible to being arrested when drunk.

Even so, to a large section of the public of this area, homeless alcoholics stood out clearly. So noticeable was their presence in the foreground, the community, streets, markets, entrances to blocks of flats, underground car parks and in particular, their occupancy of the precious green space that existed where they congregated in such numbers as to severely curtail the recreational outlets of local inhabitants. So much so, that public attitudes reflected pity at their plight, frustration as attempts to help them seemed futile and rage at their presence which seemed ubiquitous.

Finally, they were seen against the background of hostels and confused with the largely respectable residents of such accommodation to such an extent that the prevalence of alcoholism that undoubtedly existed within this group was by extension applied to the largest of all the groups, the hostel-dwellers. Given the existence of these two groups within the area, the one being alcoholics in treatment, the other, practicing alcoholics, prevalence of alcoholism was identifiable but was of limited value, since these groups represented a considerable minority of the gross hostel population. Therefore, it was necessary that the researcher, in seeking to identify prevalence of alcoholism, should study the largest group within the area and arguably, a static one, certainly a heterogeneous one, which by virtue of its size could indicate prevalence of a measurable extent. Such prevalence, should it exist, could then be examined and an assessment made of its size, distribution and the severity of alcohol related problems within that population. Furthermore, a shift from arbitrary notions of the prevalence of alcoholism, aided by precisely directed research, to a focus of reasonably accurate judgement could be affected, from which might flow crucial considerations in planning a proper and adequate response.

The hostel-dwellers of Tower Hamlets had characteristics attributed to them about which it is easy to generalise. But convenient labels like dossers, social security scroungers, chronic boozers, work-shy and con-merchants, had a habit of being retailed until they had a currency of fact so that the real identity and character of such individuals became submerged beneath an irremovable stigma.

The Hostel-dwellers of Tower Hamlets were not insensitive to this labelling, but did not combat it. They did not form themselves into Residents Associations and pepper the press with corrective rejoinders for the way they were described. Rather they retreated into themselves and resisted any penetration into their privacy, which was not tradeable for the necessities of survival. In keeping with this desire for and pursuit of anonymity, it was the general practice of hostel managements to accommodate the hostel-dweller with the minimum of personal information being recorded. Such information obtainable could be paraphrased as of the name, rank, number variety with the mutual avoidance of "pack-drill". So, it was quite common for hostel-dwellers to occupy a particular establishment for many years and hostel staff, however interested in their welfare and seeing them every day, knows virtually nothing about such individuals.

This lack of "hard" information, which could reveal useful profiles about age, health, social and personal circumstances of the hostel-dwellers, weakened hostel managers' attempts to portray their residents in any form of factual light for public consumption. Besides, such attempts were often viewed with suspicion as being alloyed by considerations of attracting sympathy and charitable income and justifications for each hostel's *raisons d'tre*. In any event, the hostel-dwelling population was regarded by the general public as a mass of drifting people, without origins in the area, regularly represented in the magistrates courts and with little claim on social and civic amenities.

It was opportune then, given the plethora of unsatisfactory knowledge and poverty of facts about the hostel-dwellers in the area, that a method of survey, which would primarily seek to establish the prevalence of alcoholism in the hostel population, could at the same time elicit a series of social, demographic and health profiles concerning this population, which hitherto had not been available. The survey accumulated a body of information concerning the hostel-dwellers, which is acknowledged in a general way, but for the purposes of the survey was of specific relevance to a proportion of a sample of hostel-dwellers among which the prevalence of alcoholism was identified.

In the area in which this survey was conducted, seven hostels were identified and designated as non-specialist. That is to say, that although such establishments provide shelter or accommodation for problem drinkers, they are not specifically maintaining a service for this group, but providing accommodation for a diverse population of men and women.

Victoria Home:	223 beds		Male
Booth House:	200 "		"
Middlesex House:	175 "		"
Riverside House:	102 "		"
Hopetown Hostel for Women	153 "		
Tower House:	657 "		Male
Providence (Row)	44 "	35	Female.

The Research Brief was firstly, to establish-the total number of beds in each hostel provided for the use of clients. Secondly, to seek and having obtained permission from hostel managements conduct an anonymous random one in ten survey of all the beds in each of the designated hostels: one in five for women residents. Thirdly, to identify and interview by means of a questionnaire, every co-operative occupant of the randomly, selected beds in each of the designated hostels, and record any refusals or non-contacts.

Fourthly, with the purpose of identifying prevalence of alcoholism within the hostel population, elicit response to a questionnaire designed to indicate respondent's addiction to alcohol. Finally, to collate and analyse the information obtained.

Preparatory work for the Survey commenced on 20th August 1979. On that day, I obtained an interview with the senior hostel management officer of the Salvation Army of the area based in the City of London. He checked my credentials from the Alcohol Studies Centre and after questioning me thoroughly as to the reasons for the survey I was given permission to sample in the five *Salvation Army Hostels*. The Brigadier expressed an interest in the eventual findings of the Survey and I agreed to his request that the result be sent to him in due course.

I then sought an interview with the Manager of the commercial hostel, Tower House situated in Whitechapel, Stepney, who told me on the telephone, that there was not much chance of my being allowed to sample in his hostel: "Besides, the residents won't talk to you!" I obtained an interview with him two days later, and by the end of a delicate half an hour in which I parried all his attempts to dissuade me, obtained permission to sample in the hostel. His main arguments were that the exercise would serve no useful purpose; the hostel was not for alcoholics; the men would not co-operate or avoid me; and, we've had "people from the News of the World here before!"

My bona-fides were in order: I had written to him while waiting for our interview enclosing copies of the questionnaires and confirming the appointment. My main points were that the survey was absolutely confidential, had nothing to do with how the hostel was maintained or run, and was not a study of residents' attitudes to the accommodation, himself or his staff. Besides, my being allowed into the hostel would surely prove or disprove his fears. I also assured him that the results would be conveyed to him. "Very well then" he said ominously, "you can use a corner of the billiard room!" About the same period, a letter that I had written to Providence Row Night Refuge, Spitalfields, managed by The Sisters of Mercy, brought a telephone call the following day, saying that I could start there any time I wished.

I decided to commence the Survey in The Salvation Army (*Victoria Home*) Whitechapel Road, on 27th August, a Bank Holiday Monday. On the previous Friday, I visited the hostel during the day and introduced myself to the Captain-in-Charge. He was very friendly and helpful, adding that "You'll be lucky if the guys will talk to you!" a recurring theme of all the hostel staff in each hostel.

There were many variations on this theme:

The Questionnaires:

"You'll get them stuffed up your nose".

"They are too sensitive".

"The blokes will resent you implying that they are alcoholics".

"All you'll get is lies".

My Persona:

"They'll suspect you're from the Social Security" - *The Police."*

'*A plant by the management: "Nobody's ever done it before and got away with it!"*

These opinions were added irritants to my anxieties that I might fail, but were minor compared to the major anxiety which nagged me as I planned my approach to the survey. I was sure about the strategy of the survey but was uncertain about tactics. Surveys of this kind often involve some form of transaction, for example, a fee; a reciprocal service to the respondent for that rendered to the information seeker, perhaps a packet of cigarettes. Apart from seeking to establish an immediate rapport with people who would feel threatened or suspicious of me, I wanted the interviews to be a transaction with possibly, a trade-off.

Both questionnaires showed possibilities whereby the interview could be a transaction. In the primary questionnaire, a question about housing gave the interviewer opportunities of giving advice which the respondents might appreciate. In the secondary questionnaire, provided it was relevant to the respondent, there was a clear attraction to the respondent to learn his score on a feedback from the interviewer. Both these possibilities were deficient, however, for they were dependent on obtaining the respondent's participation in the interview situation and getting them to answer the questions. Nonetheless, I realised that the strongest element in the survey's approach was the factor of anonymity. But how to make this credible to the people I would meet? What was more, how to exploit it? The first interview provided the solution.

When the Captain-in-Charge had finished talking about the difficulties I would experience, which lead to the above digression, I explained that I wished to take a one-in-ten random sample of all the beds in the hostel. He gave me the number of beds and I established in what sequence they were numbered. A proportion of these were staff beds and I identified these by number separately. As I had decided that the survey should extend throughout the hostels and penetrate to their furthermost corners, I then familiarised myself with the internal geography of the hostel by a tour with him of its height, length and breadth.

As we went along, I questioned the Captain on practices for accommodating the hostel's users which were common to his hostel and the other Salvation Army Hostels and probed for those peculiar to his own. Do you, for example, book the elderly users in a particular group of beds, - likewise, the sick, the infirm, those in employment, the "regulars" and the long-stayers? I was looking for bunching in the run of beds or clusters of categories which could mean over-sampling a particular group. No. The general practice is to let the beds arbitrarily, with an exception for the pensioners who are accommodated on the ground floor. How many? About a dozen. Is it possible, for someone to be booked in here, but not be staying here? No, you can't use this place as a postal convenience. We believe in using the beds for those who need to occupy them. That was good to know, since my brief was to maintain an undeviating one-in-ten course throughout each hostel. Certain non-contacts could considerably reduce the sample. Even so, I was later to identify "ghost lodgers" elsewhere. It was agreed that I could start on the evening of the Bank Holiday.

During the intervening couple of days, I made preliminary visits to two other hostels and in preparation for my first attempt at sampling, listed the numbered sequence of the beds in the first hostel on graph paper, denoting the staff beds. Then, on a random start from the first numbered bed, I spotted every tenth bed, circumscribing the staff beds. I was thus equipped with a simple visual plan of the bed-run of the hostel. I planned to extract these numbers and note them on a separate piece of paper for the hostel staff, but instead took this plan with me to the hostel.

On arrival at the first hostel, I gave the booking clerk a note with the numbers of the residents I wished to see. I waited for about an hour as different staff were establishing which people were in and obtaining them for me. I had been allocated a small office with a desk and through the window I could see the men arriving and moving back and forth in a small yard outside. From time to time, they peered at me through the window and went away. I arranged the chairs so that I could sit alongside the people I hoped to interview. At last, my first subject arrived.

To my consternation, the staff members introduced him to me by his name - despite my having made it clear earlier that I did not wish to know the names of anyone and went away. I greeted the man in a friendly manner, shook his hand and introduced myself, and at my invitation, he sat down beside me. I then explained my purpose, saying that I am a student who is writing a paper about men and women who live in the various hostels roundabout, and that the management of the hostel had allowed me to approach a number of men in this hostel and record their answers to a number of questions anonymously. The man then agreed to be interviewed provided that I could prove that his involvement was anonymous. I explained that it was unfortunate that his name had been disclosed on his introduction to me and that it was an accident, besides I had already forgotten his name.

Then, the bed-plan, which I had on the table in front of me ready to tick off his number, proved to be useful. I showed it to him and explained how it was devised. Picking him out, I said, was rather like sticking a pin in a list of horses from the racing card out of today's paper, or making a selection in the same way on the pools coupon. The idiom of this explanation was quite satisfactory. The interview was then completed successfully.

So, right at the beginning of the survey, I had a means of allaying respondent's fears, that they could be identified by name. Here was a kind of transaction - at best, a very useful trade-off. In all subsequent interviews in this hostel and throughout the survey, I showed each respondent the sampling frame and it was a most effective working tool during the first crucial minutes of each encounter. I completed sampling in the first hostel in four nights.

The second hostel (*Booth House*) Whitechapel, Stepney, was easier because its occupants were occupied in individual numbered rooms. As it was next door to the first hostel, I had made my preparations in much the same way as described for the first hostel, by calling there in the evenings, in the intervals of waiting for respondents to turn up in the first hostel. However, despite having checked my sampling frame with the booking clerk and his confirming its accuracy, a procedural difficulty was averted.

In contrast with the first hostel, where I was static and the staff brought men to me, here I was allowed the freedom of the building and I walked about knocking on the doors of the people I wished to see. On my first round, I got no response from the first ten possible and at the eleventh room found the occupant in but he occupied a double room. He was not amenable to being interviewed as he was just going out to an evening job.

Returning to the reception office and establishing that there were a number of double rooms, I recorded their numbers and went home and drew up a fresh sampling frame, which included the double rooms and adjusted the one-in-ten sequence to sample individual occupants throughout the hostel. Subsequently, in those rooms with two occupants both in at the same time, my respondent arranged for me to call back at an appointed time, or his room-mate excused himself for the duration of the interview. It took a fortnight to interview the bulk of this hostel's sample and the remainder in one's and two's over the six weeks duration of the survey. This was the only hostel where I operated on a call back pattern as it was the highest grade hostel with long stay residents. In the other six hostels, I stayed in each and completed its sample before moving on.

The third hostel's (*Providence Row*) sample was obtained on one visit. This was a Night Refuge for men and women where the occupants do not usually go out in the evening after being admitted; a custom peculiar to that centre, whereas in all the other hostels occupants book in and go out for the evening, returning to sleep later or after midnight in some cases. At the Refuge, I was allotted the visiting doctor's surgery for interviewing the women, and an empty dining-room for the men.

The first night at the fourth hostel (*Middlesex Street*), situated in the Petticoat Lane area, was the most depressing. The staff member set the tone: "There's not much chance of getting blokes here!" indicating that my presence could start a mass exodus of the occupants. I checked my sampling frame with him and then there followed a difficult discussion between him and the Officer in Charge as to who should unlock the office which I had been allocated. That settled I was wished the best of luck. The staff member then said: "Right, they're in there!" at the same time opening a door. I went through and entered a large room where about 150 men were sitting watching television. I sat there for about an hour: from time to time men came over to me wanting to talk; mostly running down the hostel. Eventually, I summoned up the courage to make an announcement standing on a chair before the assembled men. The television drowned much of what I said and the rest was punctuated with shouts of:

"Get 'em off!" or

"Get 'em off!"

"Get your hair cut!"

"Send 'em back to the Spike!"

While I called out a series of bed numbers, my words had no effect whatever, so I sat down and wondered how am I going to complete my sample here? After about half an hour, a man came up to me and identified himself by his bed number, but he did not want to answer questions. I left the hostel thoroughly dispirited.

Having returned to the hostel earlier the following evening, I met a different member of the staff who said I could go up to the dormitories. My first contact told me to go away and not bother him. He thought I was from the Housing Department, but when I explained my purpose, he agreed to be interviewed. He turned out to be very interested in the survey. He took away my list of bed numbers, saying:

"I'll find these blokes for you!"

Very soon, I could hear him shouting out bed numbers in the common areas, which resulted in a steady stream of respondents coming for interview. I completed sampling in the hostel in five nights.

The next hostel (*Garford Street*) Limehouse, Poplar, was notable for a bad start. There, the Officer in Charge put me in the chapel, which doubled as a television lounge for the hostel staff, who were evicted to accommodate me. I waited for an hour and a half before seeing a respondent. During that time, the door opened about thirty times and I was glared at by different men who were obviously staff. Eventually, the Officer returned and said that he was now going off duty but he had obtained a number of men who were waiting to see me. After he had gone, the staff re-possessed their lounge and when I enquired about the men who were waiting to see me, I was told that they had got fed up with waiting.

Next evening, the staff member on duty, who told me that "thanks to The Salvation Army" he was a recovered alcoholic, was very keen to help. As it was a fine summer evening and there was a garden with benches in the grounds of the hostel, I suggested that I could do the interviewing on one of the benches there. This was very acceptable and the sample was concluded, in this fashion, in five nights.

One of the men was a mystery to the staff and it was suggested that it would not be worth seeing him as he never speaks to anyone and goes to bed very early. I was allowed to come back and see him in the early morning before he went out but could not communicate with him. The Major-in-Charge said he believed the man to be an East European and that he was an out-patient at the local psychiatric hospital. It was agreed that I could return again with someone I know who speaks several East European languages. This was done about a week later, but my friend had no success in communicating with him.

The initial contact with the (*Hopetown Street Hostel*) Stepney, was not very inviting. In a telephone conversation with the Major-in-Charge, I was told that people like me (research workers) are a nuisance and that they "frightened the ladies." The Major agreed to see me by appointment and I wrote to her in the meantime. Subsequently, I met the Major at the hostel - a grim and intimidating place from the outside - which belied the warm, sensitive and protective nature of its custodian. I was given every assistance by herself and the staff and completed the sampling in five evenings. I was told that many of the residents were secretive and had lived in the hostel for many years with minimal communication between them and the staff and that I was to expect many refusals. In fact, I found the women to be very friendly and keen to stay and talk about their lives. Some of them did indeed refuse interviews to the staff but found their way to me, saying that they did not wish the staff to know about it.

There was a distinct undercurrent of anxiety and uncertain anticipation in the residents I met, as the hostel was shortly to close and the residents would move to a newly built hostel in the neighbourhood. Many of the residents have lived in the hostel for over 30 years and it was both a sanctuary and home to them. One woman would only be interviewed if she was accompanied by her sister. This was agreed to on the proviso, by her sister, that she be interviewed also. They had lived as devoted companions in the hostel for nearly thirty years, having arrived there with their aged mother who lived with them for ten years until her death.

Another lady had no objections to being interviewed so long as I did not write down the answers to the questions. "People never listen to me. All they do is writing down what I say and never tell me what they're writing about me". I asked her if it would be alright to write her answers later and she said "Yes, as long as you don't write while I'm talking to you!" Other residents, not in the sampling frame, insisted on seeing me, "*Just for a chat and a smoke...*"

Tower House (*Fieldgate Street*). Work began here, from a corner of the billiard room and the staff member on duty the first evening told me that I was to stay there and not move around the building as it was too risky. He felt that if I moved around the corridors and a room was left open and something stolen I would be suspected of stealing. I was thus unable to interview anyone. The following evening, the manager gave his permission for me to have the run of the hostel, telling me that two days before; his assistant had done a moonlight with the staff's wages.

It took 20 consecutive nights to complete the sample with some contacts being made as late as 11.30 p.m. All interviews were conducted in the rooms of the residents. The bulk of refusals being made through closed doors. Early on in this sampling procedure, I found that I was getting a high level of non-response at knocking on doors, and although I established from the booking office that all the rooms in the sampling frame were let, I was concerned that a number of them might not be actually used by the men who had booked them. So, I observed the way in which residents collected their mail. It was common practice in Tower House for a list of names of the recipients of mail to be displayed and men on production of identity and bed-ticket collect their mail at the booking office.

A member of staff had told me that some men do not live in the hostel and I watched with him as men came through the front door of the hostel, identified themselves at the booking office, collected mail and went out immediately. So I established that the "*ghost lodger*" does exist. Over a period of about a week, I observed eleven men use this system and money changed hands. The reasons for this poste-restante are intriguing but specific only to this survey in that I could have "lost" a number in the sample, were it not for the fact that all refusals in this hostel were either face to face or through a closed door.

The methodology of the survey determined an undeviating one-in-ten random technique. This was adhered to throughout. The validity of that rests solely on the integrity of the researcher. The natural temptation to force the pace of data collection by deviating and taking anybody as a respondent was, it is true, experienced, as the researcher adjusted constantly to the interactions between him, the hostel-dwellers and their environment. Two important factors in the design checked this temptation: one established its validity, the other reinforced it. Firstly, by using the sampling frame as an essential justification for engaging the respondents in the interview situation, people outside the design were of necessity ignored.

Secondly, for those respondents not interviewed in the privacy of cubicles or rooms, but occupying a bed in the dormitory, their bed ticket number was anonymously ascertained at the end of each interview. It was considered imprudent to see it earlier since the risk of losing the trust of the respondent's wish for anonymity was too great. In effect they placed their thumb over the name so that I could only observe the bed number. The survey accumulated a body of information concerning the hostel-dwellers which is acknowledged in a general way, but for the purposes of the survey was of specific relevance to a proportion of a sample of hostel-dwellers among which the prevalence of alcoholism was identified in 49% of the surveyed group with dominance in the 40-59 years age band.

A further three months were spent on preparing a Review of the Literature, writing up the survey data and tabulating the statistical analysis. Eventually, in January 1980, the Dissertation was academically reviewed and published. Copies were distributed to the hostels and placed in Tower Hamlets Public Library and the library of Queen Mary College, Mile End, University of London and The Greater London Council Housing Research Department. The project was completed, when in late spring 1980 I was presented with my qualification by *Sir Malcolm Rifkind*, Minister of State for Scotland.

In a poll of lecturers and fellow students, my Dissertation was voted best designed and the most interesting largely, because of the 18 identified and cited academic references. Some of these, to conclude this recollection, are included here as follows:

As early as 1851, *Mayhew* wrote specifically of the lodging houses in *Tower Hamlets*: "Some of these lodging houses present no appearance differing from that of ordinary houses; except perhaps, that their exteriors are dirtier. Some of the older houses have long flat windows on the ground-floor, in which there is rather more paper than glass. 'The windows there, sir,' remarked one man 'are not there to let the light in, but to keep the cold out.'

London Labour and the London Poor (4 Vols. 1861)

In the year 1855, an Irishman in East London was prosecuted for keeping a disreputable lodging house, which had housed 15 Lascars, 9 Chinese, 2 prostitutes, a poor Irish widow and two dead bodies. (David Brandon 1970).

The Decline & Fall of the Common Lodging House (1969) A Paper for Christian Action

Charles Booth, 1887, writing of the area in which the majority of hostels are situated today, observed:

"In Whitechapel, are to be found most of the common lodging houses accommodating the strange bedfellows, whom misfortune brings together, and lower still there are the streets of furnished rooms where stairways and corners are occupied by those without any other shelter."

Conditions and Occupations of the People (1886-87) A Paper read before The Royal Statistical Society in May, 1897

Most of these establishments had come into being as a result of the 1834 Poor Law Amendment Act, which severely restricted the extent and quality of statutory provision in the form of both the workhouse and the newly developing casual wards. The housed poor could obtain "outdoor relief" but the homeless poor were forced to seek shelter in lodging houses for the Vagrancy Act of 1824 placed harsh penalties on those apprehended and found "wandering abroad" without visible means of sustenance. Public drunkenness was widespread in the years leading up to 1879 when The Habitual Drunkards Act was enacted. The poor were hemmed in on all sides as the industrial revolution plunged one era into economic decline while raising another in relative prosperity. Crushed as Pelion-Punishment piled on Ossa-Poverty and the moral, penal and political systems collided in confusion the Brewing Industry flourished, particularly in East London.

"The Mile End Road, which is the great main thoroughfare through the East End from the City of London west, to the vast glades of Epping Forest in Essex, has no more conspicuous an object than the vast brewery of Messrs. Charrington and Head. From the mighty portals of this brewery, day by day, throughout the year, a never ending flood of alcohol is pouring and in those enormous vats, who shall say how many souls have been dissolved?"

All Sorts and Conditions of Men. Sir Arthur Besant (1882)

To this brewery, owning hundreds of tied public houses, producing the revenues of a prince for its proprietors, Frederick Nicholas Charrington was heir. He was born in the Bow Road on 4th February 1850. But for one incident, which occurred as he walked from the brewery, he would never have been included in the ranks of the other Colossi of the period, William Booth (1829-1912 and Thomas Barnardo (1845-1905).

Charrington recalls: "As I approached this public house, a poor woman, with two or three children dragging at her skirts, went up to the swing doors, and calling out to her husband inside, she said: 'Oh, Tom, do give me some money, the children are crying for bread.' At that the man came through the doorway. He made no reply in words. He looked at her for a moment, and then knocked her down into the gutter. Just then I looked up and saw my own name CHARRINGTON, in huge gilt letters on the top of the public house and it suddenly flashed into my mind that that was only one case of dreadful misery and fiendish brutality in one of the several hundred public houses that our firm possessed. I realised that there were probably numbers of similar cases arising from this public house alone. I thought as in a flash, that whatever the actual statistics might have been, there was, at any rate, an appalling and incalculable amount of wretchedness and degradation caused by our enormous business.

It was a crushing realisation, the most concrete unavoidable object lesson that a man could possibly have. What a frightful responsibility for evil rested upon us! And then and there, without any hesitation, I said to myself - in reference to the sodden brute, who had knocked his wife into the gutter, - *'Well, you have knocked your poor wife down and with the same blow, you have knocked me out of the brewery business.'*

"I knew that I could never bear the awful responsibility of so much guilt upon my soul. I could not allow myself to be a contributory cause, and I determined that whatever the result, I would never enter the brewery again." *The Great Acceptance. The Life of Frederick N. Charrington. (Guy Thorne 1913)*

This conversion of a Damascan impact brought enormous benefit and relief to the social effects of alcoholism in the community, which continues to this day in East London. One of the churches in the East End which, with the help of Charrington, began working with the homeless alcoholic in the neighbourhood; *The Lycet Methodist Mission of The East End Mission* has provided, through its work for this group at St. George's Cable Street, some definition of the hostel dwellers.

A Paper by *Smith R.* and *Moore D.* in 1971 examined data which they collected during a period from 1st March 1968 - 28th February 1969 inclusive. They preface their examination of 607 homeless men with the remark: "We began our examination... in an apparent vacuum, without any previously collected information or any sound assumption to work from." This is an important observation, for although *William Booth* had responded to the catastrophic conditions that prevailed in East London by providing hostels, no documentation appears to be available in any readily accessible form, about the hostel-dwellers. Yet, Smith and Moore found that in their 607 men, "51% slept rough the night, preceding their visit to the Day-Centre while 67% slept in a hostel or private accommodation on the night, preceding at least one of their visits. "The majority, 90% of their sample, was shown on analysis of % of visits to have used Salvation Army Hostels in East London. It was noted "that on average our men sleep rough less often than they sleep in hostels".

A Report to the Director of Social Services, London Borough of Tower Hamlets. A No Fixed Abode publication. (1973) Richard Smith.

Chapter 6 – The Politics Of Hunger

Elsewhere, in Oxford for example, a homeless man, convicted of begging, has been served with an ASBO - anti-social behaviour order - which, if breached, can mean summary imprisonment. The beggars, as if they ever were, are now no longer welcome. In many ways, their current situation has been determined by those among their number who have earned the repute of being super-beggars. These interlopers, having infiltrated the vagrancy scene, studied the range of artful dodges that begging requires, and converted those skills into a science. So much so, according to newspaper reports, individuals have been identified and admitted to making a handsome and regular income from begging.

It is possible that the Conservative Mayor of Assisi is courting a reaction and attempting no more than what may prove to be a politically expedient temporary clearance. His action has quickly attracted Vatican comment:

"Saint Francis is the saint of the poor and his teachings are still relevant. As a Christian, I don't understand it," said Renato Martino, president of the Vatican's Pontifical Council for Justice and Peace. Begging is not a crime. I don't understand why it has to be banned by adopting a law. Even if some people take advantage, helping those who are in need is always a good thing to do."

The head of the Assisi Franciscan monastery, Vincenzo Coli, said in a statement carried by - La Republica - the city's principal newspaper: St. Francis *"Recommended recourse to begging only when it was not possible to sustain oneself through work"*.

When I worked with homeless people in London during the 1960s, a rogue element in the Metropolitan Police - quite unofficially - took to nightly round ups of homeless beggars in central London and transporting them in vans to Epping Forest on the fringe of the metropolis, miles away, where they were left stranded. A similar practice was being pursued in China as a branch of street cleaning in preparation for the 2008 Olympic Games.

Periodic clearances of beggars have been undertaken by civil and civic authorities for centuries. In the plays of William Shakespeare, instances of beggars being chased beyond the city walls occur frequently, when a King or Emperor arrives in a city. In medieval times, concessions were made when a token beggar was retained to have Christian charity publicly bestowed upon him by the monarch. This act was usually performed as a ceremonial event carried out publicly on the steps of the Cathedral or principal church.

Perhaps the time has come for all municipalities to designate a token beggar. They could be situated on a Town Hall Steps, on a rota basis and their income carefully monitored. Any excess beyond a day's Income Support would be placed in a designated fund and used for general relief by local charities providing rehabilitation, resettlement and long-term housing support. This statutorily approved beggar could be suitably clothed to attract visibility and generously badged with supporting business logos and those of charitable organizations.

In my charity raising days, I was no less a beggar than those I acted for, as I petitioned for homelessness funding causes in the sumptuous board-rooms and indulged the hospitality of the City Livery Companies. The thoughts of George Orwell are worth recalling from *"Down and Out in Paris and London"*:

"Money has become the grand test of virtue. By this test beggars fail and for this they are despised. If one could earn even ten pounds a week at begging, it would become a respectable profession immediately. A beggar, looked at realistically, is simply a business man, getting his living, like other business men, in the way that comes to hand. He has not, more than most modern people, sold his honour; he has merely made the mistake of choosing a trade at which it is impossible to grow rich."

Saint Francis of Assisi

Has it got all too easy in Assisi?
In centuries past, it wasn't easy
for Saint Francis of Assisi:
he had to beg to live
reliant on those who give
alms, hoping for exemption
from Hell and its redemption.

What was over, the fair
beggar Friar gave away
for others to share.
He built a shrine there:
pilgrims came to pray
in Assisi and imitate his ideal

In a Declaration of real
politic, Mayor Claudio
Ricci has banned all
begging and doing so
has caused a major row.
Now Poverty is a vice.

The head of Assisi's
Franciscan monastery
Vincenzo Coli,
says that Saint. Francis
"Recommended recourse
to begging only when
it was not possible to
sustain oneself through work".

Give to the one
and not the many.
Blessed are the needy!
Banished will be the greedy!

Anthony Brady

Chapter 7 – A Caviar Champagne Christmas

I helped organise the OPEN CHRISTMAS, a three-day fest of soup, mince pies, sausage rolls and blankets, circa late 60's early 70's. Today, it is a very efficiently run ten-day seasonal event, which highlights and responds to relieving the lonely Christmas conditions of homeless people; not only in London but in nation-wide venues also. What was once a London ad hoc effort to provide basic food, clothing and warmth as a brief respite for people, who slept rough, is now a highly organised Charity - CRISIS - providing high standard food, baths, medical care, housing help and advice.

Twenty five years ago, a small group of mainly key church movers and shakers in the London homelessness field would meet in late September to plan what was then known as *Crisis at Christmas*. So it was that I was invited to join Rev. *David Moore* – Director Bow Methodist Mission; *Richard Smith*, Director No Fixed Abode – an umbrella group of homelessness agencies; *Rev. Eugene Morse* – East End Methodist Mission; *Rev. Malcolm Johnson*, Vicar of St Botolph's Church, Aldgate, and Church Army Captain *Terry Drummond*. A fellow layman, *Pat Logan,* founder of UNLEASH*, participated as consultant adviser.

Quaker Action supporters, members of the Salvation Army and volunteer nurses from the main London Hospital Nursing Schools as well as the Metropolitan Police cadets were drafted in. *Caspar Werley*, a monk, was seconded from his monastery to command a team of lay volunteers and direct the whole operation.

Caspar delegated various fund raising aspects to me, and I was rostered for work on Christmas Eve in 1977. Miracles were performed over a number of months and Crisis at Christmas was ready to open in St. Mary's Church – now The Tradescant Centre – next to Lambeth Palace. Long before the church doors opened, I passed a half-mile queue forming alongside the Palace and stretching down as far as St. Thomas's Hospital and County Hall where Capital Radio had set up a temporary studio.

I had been assigned to contribute to a broadcast about Crisis at Christmas with *Jim Horne* – charismatic founder of St. Mungos, Or-

ganiser of nightly Soup Runs and master of empty buildings acqui-
sition as shelters for homeless people. The Director of CHAR –
Campaign for Homeless and Rootless People – and tireless cam-
paigner – *Nicholas Beacock* spoke also. The tailpiece of the discussion
was the opportunity given to contributors to make a direct appeal
specific to each represented charity. I appealed for footwear and
clothing for Providence Row Night Refuge. Next day, tons of both
requirements were delivered: a particularly unusual gift was hundreds of unused blue Metropolitan Police issue shirts – without col-
lars.

When I got to St. Mary's later that night, the pews were stacked
ceiling high against the walls and the floor space packed with sheltering "dossers" – a politically incorrect word now – but that was
what they called themselves then. Indeed, *Ted Eagle* founder of
PROD – Protection of the Rights of Dossers – was a helper along
with other co-workers. I attended Midnight Service, celebrated at
the raised holy end by Malcolm Johnson assisted by Caspar. Down
in the darkened well of the church, hundreds of homeless people
sprawled on mattresses, watched over by mainly women workers.
The glow from the fags being surreptitiously smoked winked back
up at us as the service progressed. Just before the Collect, a man
rose from his mattress: mounting the steps he then sat himself down
on what would have been the Archbishop's Chair and intoned the
most perfect and appropriate Latin. He remained there throughout
and responded in Latin as and when. Communion was taken in
both kinds under the Anglican Rite.

Later, about one thirty in the morning, as we crept past the sleeping "Congregation" to head home, I heard a whispered: "Tony! Tony! Give us a fag!" In the gloom I recognised Laura, a woman, I,
along with many others, had often helped out in the past. I bent
down and gave her the remainder of a packet of Guards I had on
me while extracting a promise that she would not smoke them until
the morning. A dwarf, Laura stood on a sleeping figure cheek by
jowl on the floor and, all stale drink fumes, hung suspended from
my neck long enough to kiss me. Happy Christmas!

Laura was a chronic alcoholic. When no palatable alcohol was
available, she drank the "Jake" methylated spirit cut with lemonade.
A way of getting money was to allow herself to be thrown about –

the ancient pastime of dwarf-tossing practised at one time in certain East End Pubs. Four years later, a policeman, an acquaintance, the Limehouse Coroner's Officer in fact, told me that she had been murdered in a Wapping "Derry" a derelict house. Her special friend was eventually successfully resettled. See "Helen Goes Home".

For many years, I was very close to the street homeless of London's East End. Indeed, I was so familiar with their ways and knew their real names: *"Scouser"* Bob, *"Brummie"* Dave, *"Galway"* Mick, *"Scrumpy"* Jock etc., who usually sufficed among themselves. Others, murder squad detectives, used to visit me at Providence Row Night Refuge and asked me to help identify dead people. I would be driven to locations, where the bodies would still be lying where they were found: in underground garages, tower block stairwells, chaotic squats, derelict houses, "skippers" and any kind of makeshift shelter. Frozen, burned, battered, - often choked when being sick in sleep, sometimes gnawed by rodents. More often than not, I would look down into their dead faces, as they were slid out on metal trays from the refrigerator at Limehouse Mortuary and put a name to them.

Few people knew that at *Bethnal Green Police Station* there was a unique photographic *"Dossers Gallery"*. This consisted of a series of regularly updated photographs of homeless men and women sleeping rough in the neighbourhood: Aldgate, Spitalfields, Whitechapel, Shadwell & Wapping mainly. They were photographed in situ undisturbed as they slept. It saved a lot of precious police time.

One of the few comforts gained from working with homeless people was their sense of humour; often ironic, some of the best jokes were those they told about themselves. This anecdote about Crisis at Christmas was told me by a homeless man. I had asked him what he would have liked for Christmas and he replied: *"A school tie - Eton colours - Dear Boy! With two crossed cider bottles and the motto "Bibo ergo sum".*

My narrator set the scene of his anecdote thus: Crisis at Christmas three-day Shelter is ending. Hundreds of homeless people stream out to re-occupy the streets and whatever shelter is available: the worst off to avail of whatever minimal shelter they can find: Cardboard City: – packing cases at nearby Waterloo Station; Charing Station and under the bushes on nearby London Embankment or the DHSS controlled Camberwell Spike. The 'better off' will move back into in the numerous doss-houses of up to a thousand beds that warehoused the homeless in those days. The 'best off' having spent a few days with old associates living "on the ramp" (No Fixed Abode) will return to bed-sitters where life, for many, is an often lonely resettled existence.

Duffle-coated media commentator pokes microphone into face of our departing "dosser". "Here we have a typical homeless person who has spent three days with crisis at Christmas – *How was it for you?*" "*Most agreeable*" is the reply, which continues "*except that the champagne was flat, the caviar 'orf, the dancing girls never arrived and the mattresses had fleas.*"

"*So there you have it Ladies and Gentlemen, as I hand you back to the studio – there's always room for improvement. A Happy New Year to you All!*"

* *United London Ecumenical Action For Single Homeless*

A BODY HAS BEEN FOUND

"It's someone You might know!"
Said the voice on the phone,
"Can you come round?
Ring back when convenient,
On this number - usual hours".

At the mortuary a long metal tray
is slid out from the fridge:
The Attendant says "Another NFA!
The Winter's a killer!
Though no worse than usual!"

The face is revealed;
the eyelids are stitched.
"Nothing to go on -
Can you say who it is?
The rats got the eyes!"

Can I look at the clothes?
They might give a lead."
None found." is the reply.
"In the muddy conditions
they had all rotted away."

A last long look...
Then I turn aside;
the Attendant slides
the remains from sight.
In cold silence we look at
each other, our eyes say:
"It could be anybody."

Anthony Brady

Chapter 8 - The Bundle

I had planned a working Monday at home. *Beaglie*, my PA, was soon on the 'phone. She explained that a problem had come up and outlining her concerns sought my advice. I advised her to call Security and wait for me to come into the office. The telephone rang again. The voice of *Orton Whistow* - Chief Resettlement Officer at Spur House, Lewisham - was cheerful as usual. He had few reasons to be, as he described himself as "Juggling ferrets and up to his knees in alligators".

Since 1980, we had worked together on the staged closure of The Camberwell Reception Centre in Peckham, London and its replacement scheme. The Minister for Social Security, following advice from an enquiry team and pressure from voluntary agencies, had directed that this off-the-street direct entry institution be closed. Over five years it was to be run down and the emergency shelter it provided for 1000 single homeless men continue in smaller government run emergency provision hostels such as Spur House. About one third of the Camberwell residents had been re-housed in council flats spread among the 32 London Boroughs. Another third had moved to supported caring housing schemes. Many among the final third were returned to long stay psychiatric hospitals. The remaining rump was a group crudely designated "*the intractables*". Its average age was 60.

The lives of these men were lived against a background of what used to be called mental asylums, regular residence in alcohol recovery projects, prison sentences, large warehouse-type dosshouses and living on the streets. One remove from the streets and least preferred resort of emergency was the hostel that Orton was now based in. The rationale driving our work of resettlement was reduction of government institutions responsible for the welfare of homeless people and devolve their management to none government providers. The deadline for Camberwell's closure was met in 1985.

Reg Maddigan was one man among a stage army of homeless people, who were not always confined to London but moved about the country being traditionally able to get "moving on money" which could be obtained, after a long wait, at most Social Security

Offices. When I first got to know Reg, he had stayed in most of the long stay mental hospitals, which once ringed outer London. Though never charged with any offences, he was first committed during the 1950's at Virginia Water, Surrey for a suspected bomb hoax which closed Baker Street railway station. In the first wave of "community care", Reg was discharged and spent many years moving about London staying in night shelters, government reception centres and sleeping rough. A note in the Social Security papers that recorded his wanderings stated: "Reg Maddigan is a burned out schizophrenic". Reg's way of life mirrored the effects of reduction and closure of long stay institutions, governed by what was euphemistically called "*Penrose's Law*." A criminologist, *Penrose*, had correlated that the prison and hospital populations rose following the scaling down of numbers in the armed services following the Great War 1914-1918.

During the 1950's, newly discovered drugs and policies advanced by the then Health Minister Enoch Powell, stimulated the discharge of large numbers of patients from long stay hospitals. A noticeable effect was the rise in numbers of people resorting to large hostels traditionally used by working men. The nature of these places changed, and they became warehouses, where great numbers of people like Reg spent lifetimes in a neglected, deprived and desolate existence. Adapted to meet these changes, redundant Workhouses became government Reception Centres for the homeless and were situated in most major cities in the UK. These admitted increasing numbers of people, who required help from the welfare services, but were excluded from council housing because of priorities for local settled communities. Homeless people like Reg dropped through the welfare net. Sociologists, politicians and homelessness pundits seized on expressions such as "downward spiral, cycle of deprivation, casualties of treatment" and so on. Somewhere in that jargon was someone called *Reg Maddigan*.

Then, the large commercial hostels began to close. This caused a steady rise in numbers of people using emergency night-shelters run by charities. They began to be recorded as sleeping rough and the head count taken at nightly Soup Runs steadily increased. Conditions worsened at Camberwell Reception Centre, which by 1980 had become a massive human sump for all the inadequacies of welfare services. They became scandalous as staff increasingly turned on residents and used brutal methods of control prompting a law suit by the leading homelessness Charity. Closure, to head off court action, was agreed. Recently, Orton and the resettlement team had arranged a permanent caring housing placement for Reg. Reg visited it, was put on the waiting list and expressed his delight in his usual way: "thanks a bundle" or "I owe you a bundle". Soon after - he disappeared. Orton told me that Reg had "been in the news again" and that he was now discharged from hospital and directed to Spur House where he had stayed briefly but had left again over the weekend.

Some weeks ago, according to the news media, Euston Station had been brought to a halt by a bomb threat and Reg had been spotted in the crowd by the police specialist crowd watch team and "sectioned" to Cane Hill Psychiatric Hospital in Coulsdon, Surrey. During Reg's 28 day assessment stay, Orton heard that there had been a robbery at a local Bank. The money had not been recovered. As Orton had been on duty over the weekend, when Reg booked in as NFA, he had a long chat with Reg who told him about the robbery. Reg said he hadn't done it. He said that he had got all the money though and knew where it could be found. In a telephone call the Duty Social Worker at Cane Hill, told Orton what had happened.

Towards evening on the day following his admission, Reg was absent and the police were informed. At the bank nearby, the procedure for an armed demand for money was affected and one thousand pounds in notes was handed over. The robber left and was watched until he entered the dense woodland surrounding the hospital which was set on a steep hill. Night with a thickening fog was closing in.

For cost cutting reasons, the local police were over-ridden and a detail of vans packed with police officers from miles away eventually arrived at the bank. Acting on information: "It's a nutter from up the Hill" the squad fanned out and were soon hopelessly lost. Meanwhile, up at Cane Hill, news of the robbery spread among the couple of hundred or so patients in the erstwhile 1000 bed hospital. By the time the officers arrived, dozens of patients were admitting their part in the robbery. After a long search of many empty wards

Reg was discovered asleep in another patient's bed. No arrests were made.

When I got to my office - at County Hall, security staff completed opening a packet addressed to me. It contained one thousand pounds in notes still wrapped with the bank's seal. A message to me signed by Reg read: "Everything's fine, thanks a bundle". Later, the Bank sent a generous donation to a Charity hostel where Reg was soon located.

Chapter 9 – When London Trees Let Down Their Leaves

Roland was regarded as a fantasist by the other homeless men, living with him at the hostel called *Launcelot Andrewes House*, Southwark. They did not believe his stories about his exploits in the Special Armed Services. I knew better, having accessed his background thoroughly. When Roland moved into his council flat in Shoreditch, he posted the SAS logo *"Who Dares Wins!"* on his front door and was not pleased when I, involved with him as his re-settlement support worker, suggested this was unwise; it was a time when IRA bombs were going off in London. Roland was a resettlement success despite the periodic absences from his flat.

He would leave me signs that he was away such as a matchstick inserted between his front door and the frame or a tiny patch of cello tape over the Yale-lock keyhole of his flat. He showed me how to leave a message, when he was not at home, in the form of a paper javelin blown through his letter box with just enough force to land on a spot that was visible when I peeped through. If it was still there on my next visiting call and I got no reply to my knock, I would know Roland was still away.

Roland told me that as an ex-SAS man, he must always be ready for an instant recall so had to keep himself in full readiness. Oftentimes, he would de-camp to Dartmoor, in Devon and The New Forest, in Hampshire or to other remote places and live rough to keep himself in trim. A few nights in a London park was all part of the necessary exercises. A year after we agreed that he required no further support, I took a call from his local housing officer who said that Roland had been missing for over six months and his flat was re-possessed. More months passed. Then, the Coroner's Officer at Highbury, Islington asked me to come to the mortuary and identify a body that had been found in undergrowth in Finsbury Park. It was the mortal remains of Roland.

I went to the Inquest as the only person known to Roland, as he had specified me as a friend in notes found on his body: they were carefully swaddled in plastic together with his name, rank. number etc. The verdict was natural causes. Police speculated that Roland was sheltering in undergrowth and died of a heart attack - as there were no injuries to his body. Commuters on the top deck of their regular bus had alerted the park authority: they had noticed the body gradually appearing over a number of days as winds blew aside the leaves that had fallen and covered it. A sad story: but now somehow, Roland (though unidentified) in the poem *Autumn Revelation* is immortalized.

Autumn Revelation

The fallen leaves that spun in leaps
and bounds at every chattering gust
now lie trapped in rustling heaps
or whirl about as drifting dust.

These leaves that once the sound
of wind moved in whispering green
revealed those birds that found
cover in their shifting screen.

Lone in a park's summer shade
a single homeless man has found
some shelter – his bed he made
safe under bushes dry and sound.

Weeks into months he slept unseen
and squirrels peeped from drey
on sheltered form as the green
canopy thinned to brown and grey.

One Autumn day as gentle breezes flayed
the leafy blanket off the man concealed
top deck bus commuters saw revealed
the curled up body in death decayed

Anthony Brady

Chapter 10 – The Prince Comes To Plumstead

erve first those who suffer most. Abbè Pierre

Thanks to huge help from a wide variety of supporters, including most of the churches in the area, *Benny Hazlehurst*, a Minister at St. John's Church, aided by a group of planners, thinkers, movers and shakers, succeeded in buying a former Greenwich Council children's home on the "sharp end inner city" Glyndon Estate, Plumstead and converted it to accommodation for 23 homeless single people - Companions - who formed the first EMMAUS Community in London. Other EMMAUS Communities already exist in Cambridge and Coventry.

The EMMAUS response to homelessness is inspired by the *Abbè Pierre*, a French monk, who founded the first community in Paris in 1948. Rage had been the stimulant: the gendarmerie had called him to give the Last Rites to a homeless woman who had been found frozen to death under a bridge. The priest learned that only days before the woman had been evicted from her apartment and thrown onto the streets. The police told him that she was merely one of hundreds of people living rough in the city. Acting on impulse, he rushed to the Paris radio station and grabbing the microphone in a live broadcast described the fate of the homeless woman and implored the people of Paris to help him in a new endeavour to assist homeless people. He outlined his EMMAUS vision and invited listeners to meet with him in an act of solidarity at the Paris Hotel de Ville by 12 noon that day. The plea was recorded and played hourly. By midday, hundreds of Parisians made rendezvous with the Abbè; they brought food, clothing, blankets and cash pledges. The work of EMMAUS began. Today, EMMAUS is established in more than 300 projects world-wide.

EMMAUS communities work on 5 basic principles: they are open to anyone irrespective of background or belief; each member works to their ability for equal reward, food, clothing, shelter and a modest cash allowance for personal needs; the community helps others in need; there is no commitment as to length of stay; once functioning, each community is self-supporting by selling re-cycled or re-circulated household goods.

My experience of working for homeless people professionally and spent largely at its raw gritty edge, shades into the romantic. I was abandoned as a baby in Westminster Cathedral London and brought up by an organisation called The Crusade of Rescue. My personality was shaped by Sisters of the Enfield Sisterhood.

During the 1940s, charity is dispensed to a host of boys in a variety of orphanages, run by nuns in Hounslow and Enfield, London. Later, during the 1950s, my character is formed by Priests and Brothers in a school, situated in the Forest of Dean, Gloucestershire. It is managed by the Salesians - a religious Order, founded in Italy during the 1860s by an Italian visionary called *Don Giovanni Bosco*. He set up training schools for destitute boys in Turin in the 1860's and was a sort of Lord Shaftesbury, William Booth and Dr. Barnardo all combined.

When I left school at 15, I had no home to go to but this problem was happily solved by my being placed on a farm, where I worked as a pig stockman in an idyllic adolescence. In keeping with the traditional practice of abbeys and monasteries, the farm managers *Father Dan Lucy & Brother Joe Carter*, kept open house and I got to know many wayfarers and wandering migrants who took up our hospitality and lived among us for varying lengths of time. Thus, in a time of my most impressionable development, I learned to love and serve the poor, while a philosophy was encouraged to better myself, so I might be an effective instrument in influencing their conditions and be a force for social justice.

By the time I first met *Benny Hazlehurst* in the Autumn of 1993, I was embarking on an indeterminate "sabbatical" in a career that spanned work in Lourdes and a Belgian sanatorium, as a night nurse in a hospice; the civil service as a social security officer, the social work administrator for 5 years in London's oldest Night Shelter on Skid Row and 14 years in a combined government and local authority's specialist homeless resettlement team which I led as a principal social/housing officer for the past 5 years.

Benny was different from those like me, who have worked for many years in homelessness and dream of finding an overall solution to the problems of homelessness, that so dismay and continually challenge. He had transformed his dream to almost reality and was about to buy the children's home. I readily agreed to be involved in an idea "whose time had come". Presently, in September 1994, I was elected the first Chairman of the EMMAUS Greenwich Council of Management. One of my first public duties was to be the welcoming of *HRH, The Prince of Wales* to EMMAUS Greenwich official opening on Tuesday 29th November 1994.

Everything connected to the visit was planned and timed to the millisecond. For the sake of *HRH's* protection and safety I was made aware of possible dangers to the Prince and like others closely involved was security vetted. My only "recorded crime" was a penalty payment for going through a red traffic light in Shepherd's Bush, 1980.

The day came, and an early morning telephone call from *Benny* resolved all doubts that the *Abbè* might be too ill and weak to travel from France. Everything was not quite ready. The crude reality of a project still being developed would be evident. The *Abbè Pierre* had arrived from Paris during the early hours and after a couple of hours sleep was up at 5.30 am. As all vehicles were banned from the vicinity of EMMAUS, I walked about a mile from my home imagining the meeting of HRH with the Abbè as the English Dauphin meets the French Prince of Paupers.

I let myself into EMMAUS at 6.30 in the morning, wearing a boiler suit and learned that the Abbè was meditating. I eagerly awaited meeting someone - in his eighties - who I regarded as the greatest living Frenchman and though it was rumoured that the Abbè did not stand on ceremony I was not to be disappointed. I was busy pushing a broom when I was introduced to the black cloaked, bent over and almost blind Abbè Pierre by a French-speaking Companion: "Monsieur l' Abbè - Voici Le Chairman!","C'est bien. Nettoyez les fenètres!" the Abbè ordered. So, straightaway helped by several Companions, I got down to cleaning the plate glass windows. It was the usual chaos and we were never going to be quite ready in the way we wanted to be. It didn't matter as HRH wished everything to be normal without any veneer or cosmetic touches. Above all, he was keen to talk with the EMMAUS Companions. Later and now in my best suit, I waited by the Community front door with *Joe Lee*, EMMAUS Greenwich Administrator and *Benny Hazlehurst*.

Meanwhile, the couple of hundred guests including *Archbishop Runcie, Cardinal Hume, The Abbè Pierre* and *Vicky Morse, The Lady Mayoress of Greenwich,* came in through the shop side and waited in the workshops area. Hundreds of people had gathered. Two way radios crackled. Cell phones pipped. Cameras zoomed, flashed and clicked. The French TV News film unit took testing shots. The bobby by the door "I've seen it all before, sir!" cleared his throat - his white gloves stifling a sneeze.

The royal minders told me things were running late by 10 minutes as during prior engagements earlier time over-ran in Croydon at the opening of a power station in Deptford. So change of plan; "Greet HRH and instead of bringing him immediately into EMMAUS take him to meet the people".

Deafening cheers as the motorcade glided to a halt. *Prince Charles* steps out smiling, his hand outstretched. I grip it. *A very warm welcome to EMMAUS Greenwich* I say, adding, *the people await you.*

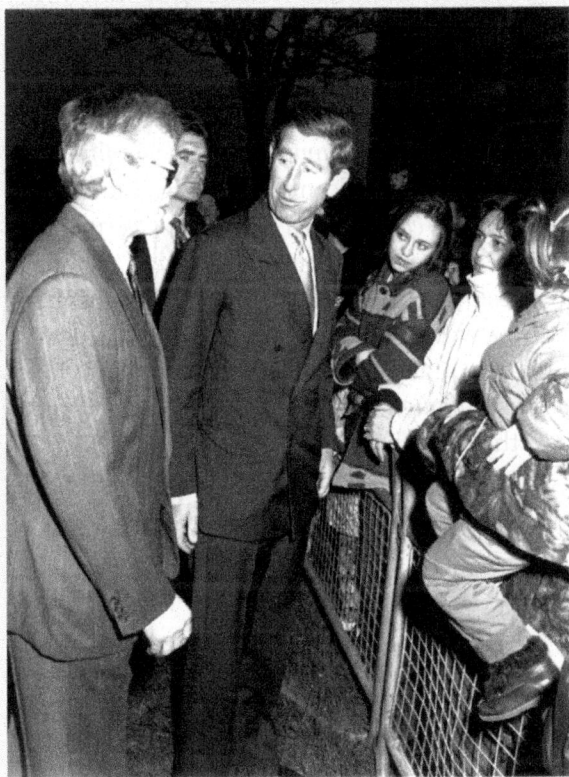

The huge crowd greets him at close quarters. Their collective voice falls on him like they say love should, with an enormous YES! To the special needs children, lined up in wheelchairs, he murmurs kind words, - to their parents words of praise, encourageagement, concern and congratulation on their devotion. People are shouting: *we love you, touch me, touch my baby.* A black man says *"come visit me royal sir."* "Where do you live?" says HRH. *"Up there, 15th floor your high and mighty."* "What's it like? Have you children?" The roar of the crowd drowns the reply.

The 25 storey block looms over us. I shout that two blocks to our right were dynamited by the Council last year. The Prince seems pleased. In the space between the lines of un-demolished concrete, the safety helmets of building site workers bob up and down under a sign: NEW FAMILY HOUSES WITH GARDENS. The crowd is roaring out its friendliness. *We want you. Please don't go away. Come back again soon.* Finally, gentle commending words to an Asian woman with her two small children and the minders steer us to EMMAUS.

Inside, Joe and Benny escort HRH to the Companion's dining room. Tea is brought: the Prince has honey in his. A Companion tells him about his former heroin addiction. The Prince shows great knowledge of the problem. *Now you've stopped don't ever start again. You will try hard, won't you?* Another relates something of his twenty years "on the road". How did it start? He could not settle after leaving the armed forces. Yes: it's so difficult.

A companion from France is introduced. HRH converses in easy colloquial and idiomatic French. *Are you happy here? Do you find what you want and need here,* he asks all the Companions. Suddenly, the Prince says to me, *"Have you ever eaten jellied eels?"* Not very often I reply. *"Indescribable! They gave me some in Croydon Market!"* Then, to the delight of everyone present, *Prince Charles'* facial expressions mimic, parody and caricature were an experience that no cartoon or Spitting Image scene could adequately capture. *"You need something decent to wash them down with though: luckily we all ended up in the pub".* Then he was away to the complete the opening ceremonials.

Postscript January 2007: A search on the World Wide Web reveals that currently, there are 13 EMMAUS Residential Projects now up and running in England - including EMMAUS GREENWICH - and 11 active EMMAUS Support Groups.

Chapter 11 – Taking The Dog To Mile-End

My lodgings could not have been more convenient to my work. They were situated directly opposite the gates of the London Chest Hospital in Bonner Road, where I worked part time weekend nights from 1963-1966. The end of terrace house consisted of a basement and three floors. My room was on the third floor back and overlooked a yard, where my landlady's children's current dog was always loose. The end wall flanked the playground of Parmiters Grammar School: a dog was a useful deterrent to pupils in search of their footballs. Even so, the dogs disappeared regularly as from cherished puppies they soon grew to be unloved mongrels and were rejected by their owners: two teenage boys and their 3 under ten sisters - in favour of yet another puppy.

Once, as the latest puppy was being fussed over, I enquired as to the fate of the previous dogs? I was told: "They've gone to Mile-End." After this had happened several times, I learned of the family's unusual dog disposal method. It having been decided that the dog had to go, one of the boys was detailed to take it on a journey by public transport. This involved taking it on a lead to nearby Central Line Bethnal Green Underground Tube station, a brief stop at Stepney Green, - then a slightly longer stop at the interchange Mile-End Station. Just long enough to cross to the platform for the return journey and command the dog to "stay" as the doors closed and the train headed back to Bethnal Green.

It was a sunny late Autumn Monday morning, as I finished my Sunday night duty at the hospital. Out of habit and the need of a short walk, I called at McDowells, the newsagents, for cigarettes and the morning paper, which were kept by for me. "*Mac.*" the owner, told me that he was going away for a few days and that a relative from North London would be minding the shop. My smokes and paper would be kept for collection as usual. Later, as I let myself into my room, I noticed a note in my landlady's hand had been left under the door. "*We have all had to go up to Birmingham for a funeral. Could you look after the dog? It's a bit wild - keep it on the leash. It's going to Mile-End when we get back. Thanks.*"

I picked up the two ten bob notes left with the message. I slept until about five and woke to the sound of a dog barking. As the butcher's shop was at the end of the street, I did not take long to collect the standing order of mixed bones. By this time, it was dark as I let myself into the unlit basement, leaving the street door open to let in some light. The dog was tethered by its leash in a cubby-hole. I let it free to its feed which it ignored as it jumped up at me then ran past me along the passage out of the door and away up into the street. I grabbed the leash and took off after it.

I did not have to go far as the sounds of a dog fight led me round the corner into Approach Road. At about fifty yard's distance two dogs were like hungry wolves tearing into each other; between the parked cars and into the road they struggled. A weak light filtered through the great plane trees that lined the road on either side. Then a man, who I took to be the other dog owner, aimed a kick landing his boot on my dog's most tender parts. The fight was over as my dog writhed and howled in pain. Enraged and without thinking, I booted the other man with a well-placed kick in his backside as he bent over to retrieve his dog. He fell sprawling onto it while I took to my heels. When I got back to my lodgings after a long detour of the neighbourhood, the family dog was fully recovered and sitting waiting at the basement door.

Next morning, I was still shocked from the previous night's "assault" on a local dog owner and while it was still dark, I headed for the newsagents. It was opposite the church on the corner of Victoria Park Square. A customer on his way out of the shop detained me briefly: his father was a patient in the TB Wing a ward I worked on. I glanced over his shoulder into the newsagent's window and glimpsed the person in the shop behind the counter dealing with a customer. It was the man that I had kicked the night before. I retraced my steps rapidly and returned home.

I decided that the dog had to go. Turning it loose was out of the question. Besides, it would surely return to the house. I could not risk taking it out for a walk in daylight. There was no chance of me collecting my daily paper and cigarettes. Worse still, the cafe where I habitually had breakfast was next door to the newsagent. I could hardly disguise myself as the hospital Porter's Lodge was opposite my front door. The expedient of me taking the dog to Mile-End was considered briefly then dismissed. I was sorely troubled. A loud bang on the front door: the postman.

As I took the mail I noticed two policemen on the far side of the street. Could it be my house that they were peering up at? Surely they were coming to arrest me. In my imagination headlines in the East London Advertiser glared: *"Hospital nurse assaults dog walker!"*. Then the telephone rang. My landlady's husband was using a coin-box telephone and the money was running out. There was just time for him to say they would not be back for a least a fortnight.

The dog had to go, but how? No such thing as a pet's Hotline then. I decided to pass the dog off as a stray and 'phoned the RSPCA. They soon put me onto The Battersea Dog's Home. The duty person asked "could I please take it round to the police station in Bethnal Green for collection by their van?" I considered saying that it had just bitten me and that I couldn't walk. But "would a 10 shilling donation for its keep help?" I ventured. About two hours later a van came round and "the stray" was placed tenderly within by two young women wearing jodhpurs. I was invited to visit the Home as a canine Samaritan whenever I wished. My request to home a "Peter Pan" dog would certainly be considered they indicated as they drove away.

For the rest of that week, I took a long walk to distant Roman Road to buy my morning necessities and when Mac returned and queried the uncollected papers etc., I said that I had taken up an unexpected invitation to stay with friends down in Gloucestershire for a couple of days. He mentioned in the ensuing chit chat that his helper had been kicked while out walking his dog and had "reported the bastard at Bethnal Green police station!" adding that because it was so dark a description was not possible. "Someone round your way, I think…"

Before the family's return, I went over to Battersea Dog's Home and chose a charming Jack Russell/Irish Terrier cross. Happily "homed" by the time the family returned, the girls took to it immediately. Why is it a Peter Pan dog they asked?" "It never grows up" I said. It was still there 3 years on when I moved away.

Chapter 12 – Helen Goes Home

Bill Tidnam, a now ex-colleague, shouted: *"Watch out for low bridges Tony!"* as for the last time he drove away from Camden Town Hall. For the journey home to Greenwich, he had to keep the car sun roof open to prevent the tall parting-gift sapling from bending. It was a surprise team "in joke" gift, which would soon take root in his garden in Woolwich. Now, as he looked out from a window on a winter scene in County Fermanagh, Northern Ireland, he noticed the transplanted cherry tree slowly beginning to put forward new buds. He was reminded, though a decade has passed since his retirement party, of first owning such a tree and what inspired it.

He thought of the nights he had spent with members of the Soup Run or the counting groups surveying the numbers of rough sleepers. He was cheered by the fact that so many homeless people he had known had made it back from the streets to re-settled lives in the community. The crack resettlement team he had worked with for over fifteen years, had made a lasting impact on the most challenging aspects of homelessness in London and was now disbanding. Its research, Papers and action Reports had added to official wider understanding of homelessness and led to greater government resourcing towards its solutions.

One Annual Report for the housing minister had been particularly noted: he had written it with a strong human element in the context of a resettlement follow up visit and concluded it by referring to a tree as being symbolic of renewal. Nothing unusual about that: but in an official government Report? The Report went something along these lines.

From her sitting room window on a sunny day, Helen and her visitor can see a neat green: trees are in blossom and from time to time her neighbours, of just over a month's acquaintance, call friendly greetings from nearby deck chairs. A month in the country only and the cruelties of the previous autumn are fading fast. *"When we first viewed this flat"* she said, *"It was completely bare. Now it is fully furnished."* She looked about her pleased, then remarked – *"Nothing matches, but it's home."*

Since moving into her flat, Helen has returned to visit the Refuge for homeless women in Camden, close by King's Cross Station. She had been staying there and had left without saying goodbye to some members of staff "who were very special." She was struck again by the sense of menace in the streets. All the fears and horrors she first experienced, when she became homeless and slept rough in Central London, came flooding back. Helen drew comfort from the fact that within a short time she would be safely back in her new own place and that now, her life felt secure. She was close to people, whose presence was unthreatening and she looked again at the photo of herself on her recently issued bus pass: it was not a dream.

Helen remembered that this time two years past, she had at last decided to leave a relationship, which had become unendurable. Her partner of 20 years had subjected her to the worst excesses of alcohol addiction and her departure from an intolerable life on the South Coast had terrified her as she considered its speed. Same went for the distance, where she faced the full realisation of her decision as she sheltered under shrubs in Hyde Park, central London. Within hours, she had been befriended by a homeless woman, who lived more or less permanently on the streets near Marble Arch. *"Audrey"* became her protector and guide.

For a number of weeks they shared adjoining benches and guarded one another's property when necessity demanded urgent absence. Audrey taught Helen to tie her wrist to her shopping-bag-on-wheels at night and they linked themselves at a distance with string so they could warn each other if danger threatened. Most evenings, two young men on bicycles would come by and share the benches and sandwiches and cans of soft drink. One of them told her about the Refuge/Shelter for homeless women in Camden and gave her the address and drew a map. Helen was worried about leaving Audrey, who said it would be alright as the men were "Christian Quakers." Both their Samaritans promised that they would continue to visit her and keep an eye on her welfare. She learned later that they kept their word.

After a few month's staying in the refuge, Helen met a woman worker from the resettlement outreach team and three months later, was told about a flat that she had obtained through the London Area Mobility Scheme. She had chosen Orpington because it is in Kent, where Helen was born and as a child and young woman she had been happy there. From the window Toni could see into Helen's back garden.

A cherry tree, which had been struck by lightning in a storm, was recovering from what seems a terminal wound. Under the weeds that had spread profusely, Helen has discovered a once-carefully tended garden. Tenderly she has created space for the perennials that had been overwhelmed. A neighbour called at her door. It was time for her visitor to go."

Chapter 13 – In And Out Of The Police Cells

The first time I ever spoke to a Northern Ireland policemen was when I had not long driven out of Belfast Docks. Something had just pinged off the bumper of our car as we approached a check point. *"Sorry about that Sir!"* said the RUC Officer in Charge *"It wasn't meant for you!"* Just as well, because it was a bullet. Luckily for my passengers and me, it had been fired at the police from some distance away, so its force was spent. Our survival ensured that my wife, our children and myself continued to holiday in Fermanagh annually for the next twenty five years. During that time, I rarely had occasion to speak to a police officer again.

Meanwhile, the Province was experiencing horrendous troubles, while back in London where I lived, I witnessed scenes of devastation and the untold effects they had on the Irish casual workers, who worked in great numbers in the kitchens and hotels in the capital city. I worked then in the field of homelessness and was in charge of a Refuge which welcomed individuals and families who were forced out of their homes in Belfast and Londonderry. Whether they were Catholics or Protestants was not a consideration, as the response to their needs was a Christian one from the Charity, they resorted to. It was called (Providence Row) and situated in Spitalfields, close to the Bengali community in Brick Lane and a short distance from The City of London.

An offshoot of my main paid occupation was the Chairmanship of a Charity involved in the long-term resettlement of former long-stay psychiatric hospital patients in the London Borough of Lambeth. Three of our dispersed Caring Homes were situated in Brixton. It was here that major rioting took place in 1980 and, being involved in the local community, I was among community leaders and neighbourhood representatives, who gave evidence to The Scarman Enquiry.

Eventually, this pre-eminent House of Lords Judge delivered his landmark Report, which led to the introduction of Independent Visitors to police cells. This was in response to a particular demand by representatives of the black community, who documented many injustices and mistreatment - in the worst instances deaths - and rampant insensitive treatment, experienced by its members while being held in custody by Metropolitan police officers. It was only some years after that very challenging time I learned that Northern Ireland had readily adopted the Scarman Principles to policing practice and applied them locally ahead of all the representative bodies and organizations in England.

In 1997, I moved to Fermanagh and planned to involve myself in some useful community activity that I could contribute to in my retirement. As my previous voluntary experience - mainly as a social agitator against the restriction and reductions in health and public services - did not prove attractive to the Health and Library Boards that I applied to, I was happy to defer community involvement, when I obtained a seasonal and very satisfying job as a House Guide in Castle Coole Enniskillen with the National Trust until the Millenium. By that time, my increased responsibilities as a carer caused me to look out for a socially useful activity that could be achieved within the most possible flexible family time frame.

An advertisement in both the main local newspapers *The Fermanagh Herald* and *The Impartial Reporter*, led to my three year appointment as an Independent Custody Visitor in the counties of Fermanagh and Tyrone. This was extended to a further three years expiring in March 2007. During those six years, I had been a member of a team of men and women who give of their free time to make unprenotified visits - in pairs - to police station cells (Custody Suites) in Enniskillen, Omagh, Dungannon, Cookstown and Strabane.

A typical Custody Visit, if such an event exists, gets under way with an exchange of telephone calls with whomever one is paired with for the current month and a day and time is mutually set to meet. This can be nearby the police station being visited or we both drive directly to it and present at the security barrier and meet inside the station parking area. On admittance to the Custody Suite, the Custody Sergeant checks the Visitor's official identity card and if there are any persons in custody the Visitors request to see them. Some will be about to be discharged or are being processed for admission, most will be held in cells.

Having ensured there is no likely danger to the Visitors, the Custody Sergeant then escorts them to the cells. Visitors are trained to be aware that the duty police officers often have to deal with unstable, unpredictable and violent behaviour from detainees. Sometimes, the detained person is incapable due to alcohol excess or drugs abuse or asleep having tried the custody officer's patience for hours. Others are exhausted. In such instances they are seen by the Custody Visitor at the Custody Sergeant's discretion as it would be imprudent to disturb them while they are resting. No direct contact therefore is made other than observing the detainee via the cell door peep slot and ensuring they are lying in a safe position or placed in a none-hazardous posture, having regard to these considerations the visit proceeds.

Then, the Custody Sergeant unlocks the cell door and, out of sight of the Custody Visitors but within their hearing, reads from a standardized cue card: "I have two custody visitors who would like to see you. They are not attached to the police. They are ordinary members of the public who are here to check on how we're looking after you. You can choose whether or not to see them. Would you like to see them for a couple of minutes? Can they look at the custody record to see how you have been treated while you have been here?" The acceptance or decline to be visited must be clearly heard as stated by the detained person.

Those, who wish to speak to the Independent Custody Visitors, are seen in their cell without a police officer present and asked to comment on the conditions of their detention. The detained person is greeted by both Visitors and aspects covering hygiene, refreshment, family contact, access to a legal representative and any medical needs are enquired about. Lastly, the detained person is asked if there is anything about their detention that they wish to raise. They are assured that any points they raise concerning their detention will be noted in the Report that the Visitors write while in the police station and copies will be sent to The District Commander, The Independent Custody Suite Visitors Administrator, one given to the Custody Sergeant with a final copy retained by the Visitor. They then exit the cell in which the detainee is re-locked.

The Visitors return to the Custody Sergeant and read the Custody Record. The purpose of the visit is not only to ascertain the present actual condition of the detainee, but overview their period of detention in respect of their rights, welfare and management by police officers, all of whom have a duty of care for the detained person. The Visitor's Report is signed by them both and the Custody Sergeant's name is included. Copies to The District Commander and Custody Visiting Administrator are envelope sealed and the Visitors leave the police station together. During that month, they will normally make two further visits to that police station on varying dates and times. Most visits are completed in half an hour.

Once a month all the members of the Visitor's eight person Team meet together to agree their pairings and destinations for the coming month. The meeting is the forum for sharing experiences, obtaining stationery and expenses forms, presenting their Reports and providing mutual support. Minutes are taken and circulated in advance of the next monthly Meeting. Every year, the team members hold an AGM and elect a Chairperson and a Secretary. Each Independent Custody Visitor is paid a 40p per mile travel allowance. An Annual Report is produced and printed. It lists the number of visits made, the number of detainees seen and the issues, raised by them and the Custody Visitors together with the outcomes. This is readily available and in the public domain.

During my period of service, I was teamed up with men and women from a wide variety of backgrounds and occupations: teachers, civil and civic servants, district councillors and business people. There is no special qualification to be an Independent Custody Visitor, but all share a common interest and purpose, underpinned by a desire to serve their community by contributing to the growth and development of a fair, transparent and publicly accountable management of people held in police custody. I served my penultimate year as Chairperson and final year as Secretary.

I did not find the responsibilities intruding on my day to day life. During the six years of my involvement as a Custody Suite Visitor, I Chaired a local Community Charity: Home-Start Lakeland; managed a French language early learning franchise business; obtained a qualification in Counselling from The University of Ulster through Fermanagh College, Enniskillen and through attendance in The Languages Department at the College, have learned to speak Spanish & Italian. I also early on became a *Trustee of Barnlee* - a home from home - in Lisnaskea for learning disabled men and women, whose monthly Management Committee meetings I attend.

I left this valuable service, confident that people, who find themselves in the custody and care of officers in the PSNI, are treated justly and fairly. I am certain also that those members of the community, who continue to serve as Independent Custody Visitors, will continue a most necessary and socially useful public commitment. I applaud both them and police officers whom I have come into contact with and recommend *Custody Suite Visiting* to anyone who is considering contributing in a constructive way to ensuring equal treatment for all. Believe me, having made 216 visits during the terms of my appointment, I can honestly state that Independent Custody Visiting really provides opportunities for a truly meaningful engagement and participation in Northern Ireland's community policing.

Chapter 14 – A Walk In The Garden Of The Mother House

The *Sisters of Mercy* in the convent at Crispin Street were a jolly lot and enjoyed a joke, so there was often sounds of laughter and amusement when I called in to see *Mother Fidelis*. "*Now I am not going to offer you a biscuit Mr. Brady!*" Everybody present laughed: we will see why later. "Anthony" was only used in personal meetings with her: "on Feast Days and Holy Days of Obligation," I would comment. Things were even more lively, whenever *Father John Cusack* was in on one of his regular visits. He was there one evening when I had just extracted another precious secret from Mother Fidelis concerning the Refuge's antiquated central heating system.

I hoped that one day that I would, at last, derive from her elephantine memory the final strand in the spaghetti of pipes that were the bane of my domestic administration. Over the years I had gradually built up my knowledge of a host of controlling levers from her and just one remained. It was proving difficult to obtain. I imagined that this woman, who had led her community for over forty years as its Mother Superior, might just divulge it in her last murmurings. I would hover and at the opportune moment enquire "*The stop-cock in Purcell House? Mother.*"

Father John was known as the *Dosser's Priest* due to his devotion to the welfare of homeless men and women and his unorthodox working hours in central London. Many of his priestly duties were embodied in his multiple activities as Chaplain to the users of *St. Mungo's Hostel*, based in the old and redundant *Charing Cross Hospital* and *The Bondway Night Shelter* in Vauxhall. He was available to the homeless at all hours. He stood in line with them in Social Security & Employment Offices, eased their way into hospital casualty departments, found beds for them in alcohol recovery projects, prayed over the men and women who died on the streets and in derrys (derelict houses) attended their burials and cremations, directed those ejected and barred from hostels to skippers (short term doss downs) and squats, - so much for the day job, which then shaded into organizing the nightly Soup Run from Bondway.

It was about this task and arrangements for that night's outing that he was calling at the convent to check that their Ford Transit van was free that evening. "How's the crack Tony! I see the Refuge is full as usual." "Sure an all. It's a freezing night, Father John, and I'm taking a few unlucky ones over in the van to Camberwell Spike wouldn't you know!" They're downstairs for supper only to be sure! "That's enough of the mock-Irish idiom I think." He was hoping to borrow the transit as the usual Soup Run one was in for repairs. We soon sorted arrangements and later that evening, we dropped off four men at Camberwell several miles away; then headed on to the disused Marmite factory off the Old Kent Road stopping to pick up a group of volunteer student nurses at St. Thomas's Hospital by Westminster Bridge. I left them off and Father John sent me away to a number of parish locations to pick up clothing donations and other comforts.

When I returned to Marmite, the contents of steaming cauldrons was decanted into large stainless steel thermos containers, loaded into the van to join the bread, donated stuff, high power torches and with Father John at the wheel and eight of his helpers in the back we went to The Bull Ring under the Festival Hall where a colony of rough sleepers lived in mainly large packing cases and makeshift shelters. "Keep a head count." said Father John. From here it was the "Stations of The Cross" he quipped, as a short distance away we called into the long redundant underground service tunnel beneath Waterloo Station. Many of the people, who gathered round the van here, were reasonably turned out as they were hostel dwellers temporarily barred because of drinking or misbehaviour or starting an early morning casual job: more often than not, in the kitchens of top Hotels such as the Ritz or Savoy.

Soon, Charing Cross Underground Station came into view. There, under its arches, most people were already bedded down on the pavements, so the nurses and their helpers went round, offering them soup in plastic cups where they lay. While Father John was making emergency admission arrangements for the most desperate cases, I drove round to nearby Embankment Gardens, where hungry people immerged from under bushes and canvas, strung between shrubs for soup and blankets. That done, Father John sent me off to Euston & Kings Cross Stations, saying picking him up later outside St. Martins-in-The-Fields Church, Trafalgar Square.

We were allowed onto the concourse at Euston, where it was mainly younger people kipping down in sleeping bags. We gave out blankets to those who needed them. Then off to the back of Kings Cross Station, where on pulling up in its abandoned goods-yard we encountered a large number of men and women, grouped near a barely alight remnant of an open fire. One of the nurses told me that "These guys (sic) are mostly dependent on alcohol and drugs! Many have died since I started out as a Soup Run helper!" Luckily we still have enough sustenance and warmth to offer them: the fittest lurched and staggered about, while others twitched or stirred fitfully where they were sprawled exposed to the elements. After searching the accessible empty boundary buildings by torch-light I left the scene with a couple of helpers on board and raided builder's skips in the area for discarded wood. We left that most desolate scene shouting "We'll be back tomorrow night!" to those gathered about a now blazing fire and headed back to Westminster.

Cruising along virtually empty of traffic streets, we met Father John walking up Whitehall. By now it was after two o'clock in the morning and he had still unfinished tasks and was unwearied. After jumping in, he crossed checked with everyone the number of people seen: "150" a *quiet* night. Then taking over the wheel, we sped away to drop off the nurses and parked up outside Kennington Police Station. I waited outside until he returned. He was visiting a man in the cells, who was due to appear in court later that morning. Frost-covered cars with whitened windscreens lined the empty streets. "Where to now John? - Shall I call you John Bosco? He's my favour-ite saint!" "Away with yee! As I have to be at Bow Street Magis-trate's Court at ten this morning, I'm crashing at St. Mungo's. See you at Carrington House, Sunday morning. I am hoping you will do me another favour. Thanks for the van. Goodnight and God Bless." I dropped him off at Coutts Bank in The Strand at about three thirty.

After Mass and Confessions in the 200 bed hostel in Lewisham Vale, Father John told me he was scheduled to give a talk to a group of The Daughters of Charity postulants next Saturday. Would I stand in for him as he had a funeral and cremation for a homeless man? I asked him what should be my topic. "I trust you to give them an interesting talk about Providence Row and the relevance of Charity in the modern world." I assumed for a moment that the Sisters would be of the community at Francis Street close by Westminster Cathedral. I gave him my OK then he said "You have to be at The Mother House in Mill Hill for 11.00.a.m. I'll let the Tutor Sister know."

The talk went well despite my introducer, after welcoming me, saying: "Of course we all know about Providence Row!" I told my listeners that my radical friends considered traditional charity with its arm's length handout approach as: "Blessing him who gives - not him who takes!" Charity being provided to the poor in this way *created dependence* and that the promotion of social justice was the true agenda. Yet I believed the Parable of The Good Samaritan was as applicable as ever and the Christian charitable approach, which had its roots in the Gospel never more relevant. I countered by arguing that the Good Samaritan not only gave "First-Aid" but left money with the Inn-Keeper for "accommodation/rehabilitation" before going on his way with a promise that he would return to check on progress.

All true Charity must be directed to eliminating the conditions of poverty and empowering both the poor and their helpers. Soup and blankets, though seen as mere sticking plasters, are the basic first-aid and the human contact offers numerous possibilities for change provided that the alternatives are readily accessible for those who are, according to the radical view, *marginalised* and *dispossessed.* Homelessness is not hopelessness but a state of transition.

Over lunch with the whole Community, an elderly nun introduced herself as *Sister Anthony* and asked if, when I was a child, I was in St. Joseph's Home, Enfield, Middlesex? I said I was and that I remembered her caring for me when I was ill in the Infirmary. She asked me not to hurry away but walk with her in the grounds as it was sunny outside. We talked and walked and rested now and again on the garden seats.

Sister Anthony told me that she recognized me immediately but initially drew back from renewing contact. She told me that she was aware of anger and bitterness expressed by boys who had been at St. Joseph's and was even more nervous when, as she put it, "intimidated by your articulate and sensitive approach to those who suffer." She asked me if I hated the Sisters who had looked after me. I said that some of them, like herself, were very kind and it was those Sisters that I chose to remember. I went on to say that I could not understand the cruelty of many of the Sisters and however hard I tried to forget them, it was impossible as it was hopeless to expect an explanation.

We sat down. Sister Anthony took hold of both my hands and looked me straight in my face. Hers was old and wrinkled yet she could have been looking at me with those same eyes, that youthful beauty and kindness which she displayed all those years ago as I lay in a bed under her care. "Our punishment now is that we can never be absolved from the terrible treatment that was meted out by some of the Sisters.

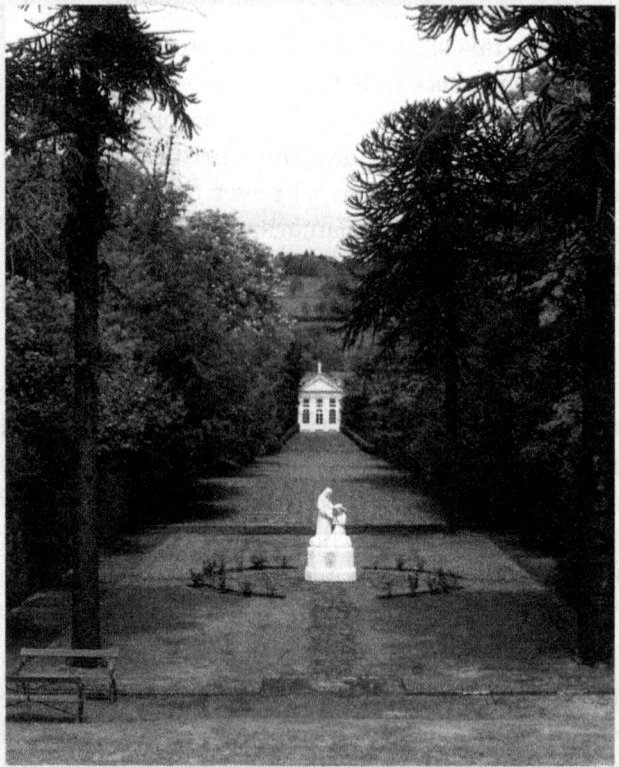

The Provincial "Mother" House, Mill Hill, London: The Garden. Photographer: Peter Comrie

I can only say that many Sisters, who because of their vocation gave up the chance of marrying and having children wanted to work on the missions in faraway countries. Instead, they found themselves in London looking after many illegitimate children, which they saw as an affront to their chastity.

It was a time of war and shortages, yet the boys in our care were in many ways privileged, compared to the children of dedicated but poor struggling married parents outside places like St. Joseph's. "*You have nothing to be sorry about.*" was all I could say.

She asked if I was married. I told her about my wife and three children. I described my times in France and Belgium. I told her about my visit to her Order's Foundation House in the Rue de Bac, Paris, and that I had seen the chair that Our Lady had sat on when she appeared to Saint Catherine Labourè. I asked Sister Anthony to tell me about herself and she revealed that she was happy in the fulfilment of her vocation. She hoped that her recent poor health would improve. I reckoned that she must be well over seventy years old.

Eventually I said "I must go soon as I have work to do with the van I came in." I have to call at Nazareth House in Hammersmith and a convent in Notting Hill on the way back but first have to go to Heathrow Airport." As we parted company, she said that she would always pray for me. I told her that one day, if I survived all the demands and pressures of my career, I would write my story and that she would be a part of it.

At Heathrow, I collected the latest full load of biscuits from the warehouse of a company who supplied them to British Airways who returned the unused packets. They had to be disposed of after transatlantic flights and were donated to Providence Row so long as we sent our own transport. It was a mixed blessing as we had had to take them although we were overloaded: hence the convent calls on the way back. The Sisters were even putting them between the slices of bread they handed out to queues of homeless callers twice a day from the doors of The Refuge.

I resolved to return to Mill Hill and Sister Anthony but learned not long after that she had died.

Whenever I see a statue of Saint Anthony
holding the baby Jesus in his arms:
the face I see that gazes at the sacred child
is not the visage of that holy monk
but yours, dear Sister Anthony.

O gentle and loving Sister Anthony
whose heart was ever full of human sympathy,
whisper my thanks into the ears
of the sweet Infant Jesus and the gratitude
of my heart will ever be yours.

Anthony Brady

Lightning Source UK Ltd.
Milton Keynes UK
UKOW06f0321100917
308736UK00007B/43/P